Cambridge Elements

Elements in Soviet and Post-Soviet History
edited by
Mark Edele
University of Melbourne
Rebecca Friedman
Florida International University

CENTRAL ASIA – RUSSIA'S NEAR ABROAD OR CROSSROADS OF ASIA?

Richard Pomfret
*Johns Hopkins University and
The University of Adelaide*

CAMBRIDGE
UNIVERSITY PRESS

Shaftesbury Road, Cambridge CB2 8EA, United Kingdom

One Liberty Plaza, 20th Floor, New York, NY 10006, USA

477 Williamstown Road, Port Melbourne, VIC 3207, Australia

314–321, 3rd Floor, Plot 3, Splendor Forum, Jasola District Centre,
New Delhi – 110025, India

103 Penang Road, #05–06/07, Visioncrest Commercial, Singapore 238467

Cambridge University Press is part of Cambridge University Press & Assessment,
a department of the University of Cambridge.

We share the University's mission to contribute to society through the pursuit of
education, learning and research at the highest international levels of excellence.

www.cambridge.org
Information on this title: www.cambridge.org/9781009507745

DOI: 10.1017/9781009507790

When citing this work, please include a reference to the DOI 10.1017/9781009507790

First published 2024

A catalogue record for this publication is available from the British Library

ISBN 978-1-009-50774-5 Hardback
ISBN 978-1-009-50775-2 Paperback
ISSN 2753-5290 (online)
ISSN 2753-5282 (print)

Central Asia – Russia's Near Abroad or Crossroads of Asia?

Elements in Soviet and Post-Soviet History

DOI: 10.1017/9781009507790
First published online: December 2024

Richard Pomfret
*Johns Hopkins University and
The University of Adelaide*

Author for correspondence: Richard Pomfret, pomfret48@gmail.com

Abstract: This Element assesses the claim that Central Asian countries hold a special position as Russia's near abroad. The region has been important for millennia, and only after conquest in the second half of the nineteenth century did Russia become important for Central Asia. This connection became stronger after 1917 as Central Asia was integrated into the Soviet economy, with rail, roads, and pipelines all leading north to Russia. After independence, these connections were gradually modified by new trade links and by new infrastructure, while Russia's demand for unskilled labour during the 1999–2014 oil boom created a new economic dependency for Tajikistan and the Kyrgyz Republic. In 1991, political independence could not be accompanied by economic independence, but over the next three decades economic dependence on Russia was reduced, and the Central Asian countries have felt increasingly able to adopt political positions independent of Russia.

Keywords: Central Asia, Russian Empire, Soviet Union, Economic Dependence

ISBNs: 9781009507745 (HB), 9781009507752 (PB), 9781009507790 (OC)
ISSNs: 2753-5290 (online), 2753-5282 (print)

Contents

1 Introduction

1.1 Central Asia and Russia

In December 1991, the Union of Soviet Socialist Republics (USSR) was dissolved, and the fifteen republics became independent nation states (Map 1). Russia replaced the Soviet flag with a historic Russian flag and reclaimed a long pre-Soviet history, as well as assuming powers, assets, and liabilities as the successor state to the Soviet Union. Since 1991, some politicians have sought to reassert Russia's influence over the other new independent states, supporting secessionist governments in Georgia, Ukraine, Azerbaijan, and Moldova (the GUAM group) and referring to Central Asia as Russia's near abroad. This Element assesses the claim that Central Asian countries have a special relationship with Russia.[1]

Before the Russian conquest, clear borders between states were absent in many parts of Central Asia. The southern border of the Russian Empire was set in the late nineteenth century when Russia occupied Turkestan and Britain and China enforced the limits of this expansion, with Afghanistan established as a buffer to the south. The borders between the Soviet republics in Central Asia were drawn in the 1920s and 1930s, approximating ethnic divisions but also suspected of being part of a divide-and-rule policy by Moscow. These borders became national borders with the dissolution of the Soviet Union in December 1991.

The region was at the centre of Eurasian history through the two millennia of the Silk Roads, when Central Asian oases were important stopping points before or after crossing the deserts and mountains on the western margin of China. Merv (Mary in modern Turkmenistan) was perhaps the largest city in the world before it was razed by Chinggis Khan in 1221. The glories of Bukhara and Samarkand can still be admired by visitors. Bukhara was a major city, boasting the world's tallest building, the Kalyan minaret, built in 1127. Later, Emir Timur (Tamerlaine, 1336–1405) ruled a large empire based on Samarkand, which his successors turned into a centre of learning; Timur's descendant Babur created the Mogul Empire that would rule India from 1526 to 1761.

In 1500, Vasco da Gama discovered the sea route round the foot of Africa that sounded the death knell for overland trade between Asia and Europe. Trade continued with Russia, China, Persia, and India, but Central Asia left centre stage in Eurasian history. The political structure, divided among a series of

---

[1] The claim has been made by Vladimir Zhirinovsky, Leader of the Liberal Democratic Party in the 1996 Russian presidential election, and by Vladimir Putin, Russia's President for most years since 2000. It is often combined with the claim that the Central Asian countries had no history as independent countries (presumably, in the Westphalian sense of a state). The fact that the post-1991 Central Asian countries had never been 'countries' does not mean that they had no history.

Map 1 The Central Asian countries after independence

emirs and khans, never matched the post-1648 European concept of a nation state.[2] Nevertheless, Central Asia's cultural, religious, and linguistic identities remained distinct and strong.

For Russia the time-path to Eurasian importance was the reverse, beginning in the 1500s and reaching great power status in the 1800s. Under Ivan III (r.1462–1505), the principality of Moscow challenged the Mongols' domination. Ivan III's rule saw creation of a bureaucratic apparatus to manage diplomatic relations and to supervise military arrangements, land tenure, and other elements of a state; landholders had to render military service and peasants had to till the land, with payment of rent and taxes supporting the state bureaucracy as well as the military (Hellie, 1971).[3] During the sixteenth and seventeenth centuries, the land controlled by Moscow was expanded. When Tsar Peter I assumed the title of Emperor of all Russia in 1721, his realm was modernizing into a European multicultural empire in which Russians accounted for only about 70 per cent of the population.[4] The expansion to the Pacific, largely in search of furs and with disregard for the indigenous peoples, had many similarities to the eighteenth-century history of western North America. After the defeat of Napoleon in 1815, Russia assumed its place with Britain, France, Prussia, and Austria as the five major powers maintaining the Concert of Europe; the Romanov empire was clearly more similar to the Hohenzollern and Habsburg empires than to France or Britain.

Incorporation of Central Asia into the Russian Empire was primarily a nineteenth-century process. Russia had been involved since the seventeenth century in the territory of modern Kazakhstan, where various groups would call on Russia for help against rival groups, but the thinly populated steppes were not a great prize. Attempts to invade the more fertile areas of Central Asia based on the two rivers flowing into the Aral Sea had failed in 1717 and 1838, largely due to distance and severe climate. Russian control over the steppes tightened and its technical edge widened. In 1865, Russian forces conquered Tashkent. The rest of Central Asia soon followed as Russian engineers built a railway

---

[2] Scott Levi (2020) documents the ongoing trade and the economic crisis of the eighteenth century. Adeeb Khalid (2021, 52–62) summarizes political developments up to the nineteenth century, when Central Asia was divided among at least eight rulers 'with varying degrees of authority and sovereignty' of which those in Bukhara, Kokand and Khorezm (Khiva) were the most powerful.

[3] Richard Hellie (1982) also documented the role of slavery, that accounted for some 10–15 per cent of the population, and the social and economic structure of Russia in the decades preceding Peter the Great (Hellie, 1999).

[4] Moving the capital to the Baltic port of Saint Petersburg signalled the intention of being a European country. However, because peasants had no attachment to the land and could be bought and sold, Russia's agrarian structure would differ from post-feudal arrangements in western Europe. Russia had also missed the Renaissance and lacked a meaningfully independent gentry or urban society.

from the Caspian to Tashkent to support first the military advance and then economic exploitation. The southern boundary of the empire was established by agreement with the British who were advancing from India; Afghanistan, with territory stretching from Persia to China, was recognized as the buffer between the two empires. Russian governors-general were installed, and Central Asia was established as part of the Russian Empire.

The above picture is clear in outline, although specifics are disputed. How backward was Central Asia before the Russian conquest? The three madrasahs of Samarkand's Registan – one of the world's most magnificent squares – were built in 1417–20, 1619–36, and 1646–60; prosperity clearly did not end in 1500. The local rulers were despotic and did not treat Europeans well (military agents were executed and captured Russians were enslaved), but the economy was not moribund. Russian military actions against the territories of Khiva or Bukhara were unsuccessful and the military breakthrough came with the capture of Tashkent, a commercial but not a political centre. Why did Russian conquest occur when it did? Central Asia was known to be well-suited to growing cotton: did the timing of conquest, coinciding with the American civil war, reflect a response to potential shortage of imported cotton for Russia's textile mills, or was it part of colonial expansion that for western European countries was centred on Africa?

Russia's treatment of Central Asians over the fifty years after 1865 was quite different from the harsh treatment of the inhabitants of Siberia or the Far East. During the half-century of Tsarist rule, Russia's principal economic interest in the governate of Turkestan lay in securing cotton for textile mills in Russia, and this was supported by transport, financial, and administrative infrastructure. The traditional society was largely untouched as Europeans lived in separate areas and religious law continued to operate in Muslim communities. Although some Central Asians were included in administration and business, the Central Asian and European areas retained their separate appearances, religion, and language. Russia linked Central Asia by rail to the Caspian and to Moscow and used those links to promote economic integration, especially through cotton, but there was little explicit attempt to change the culture or the local administration of the native population.[5] This would change after the Bolshevik revolution and creation of the Soviet Union as a multicultural society with a universal ideology.

---

[5] Communication links were established slowly. The telegraph reached Tashkent in 1873. The railway from the Caspian reached Tashkent in 1898 and was extended into the Ferghana Valley. The direct line to Orenburg in Russia was completed in 1910. Apart from expansion of cotton, agriculture was transformed by the introduction of new crops such as potatoes, tomatoes, and beets.

The connection with Russia became stronger after the creation of the USSR when the Central Asian countries became integrated into the centrally planned economy, with railways, roads and pipelines all leading north to Russia. The degree of economic dependence was greater for Kazakhstan, due to proximity to Russia and the large non-Kazakh population in the northern farms and in mining communities, than for the southern Central Asian countries. Soviet commitment to modernization led to major advances in education, healthcare, housing, pensions, and other social support. The Great Patriotic War of 1941–5 contributed to a sense of Soviet citizenship, but in this multicultural society simultaneous identities were possible. Central Asian identities were reinforced by the creation of five ethnically defined republics in which the titular language had status alongside Russian and where the political leader was normally from the titular ethnic group.

After independence in December 1991, the republic leaders transformed themselves into national presidents, emphasizing the status of the national language and the role of Islam. Specifics varied from country to country, with the religious connection stronger in Uzbekistan and Tajikistan. In Uzbekistan, Islam Karimov took the oath of office as national president on the Koran. Tajikistan was the only one of the five countries in which the transition to nation state was not peaceful, and religion played a part in the civil war. Kazakhs, Kyrgyz, and Turkmen had a more nomadic history with weaker religious identification, but new national mosques were approved by the Kazakh and Turkmen governments.

Economic independence was more difficult than assertion of cultural identity. Transport and other economic links to Russia were strong in the Soviet economy. Some links were easier to change, and some were changed by new infrastructure, but many physical links remain important. Russia's demand for unskilled labour during the 1999–2014 oil boom created a new economic dependency for Tajikistan and the Kyrgyz Republic, as remittances became a significant part of national income. In sum, political independence could not be accompanied by economic independence after 1991.

Over the next three decades, economic dependency on Russia was reduced, and the Central Asian countries have felt increasingly able to adopt political positions independent of Russia. In 2008, none of the countries recognized the independence of Abkhazia or South Ossetia, despite Russian pressure to do so, and none recognized Russia's claim to Crimea in 2014 or to five provinces in eastern Ukraine in 2022. Since 2018, the five Central Asian presidents have held annual summits (apart from 2020 when COVID prevented in-person meeting). They have also established a practice of convening as a group, christened the C5 +1 format, to meet leaders from India, the European Union, China, and the United States, as well as Russia.

1.2 A Roadmap

The central purpose of this Element is to assess the degree to which their shared experience with Russia in the Tsarist Empire and Soviet Union has shaped the economic and foreign policies of the five Central Asian countries and their relations with post-Soviet Russia. The argument in Section 2 is that incorporation into the Russian Empire in the fifty years after 1865 led to exploitation of Central Asia for its cotton and to immigration of settlers from elsewhere in the Empire, without significantly changing Central Asian society. By contrast, the Soviet experience substantially changed Central Asia, raising material living standards and providing universal education, healthcare, and other social services. It also created economic dependence as physical infrastructure of railways, roads, pipelines, and other networks all led north from Central Asia to Russia, and as Central Asian production was incorporated into supply chains reliant on other Soviet republics (primarily Russia) for inputs and for markets.

The economic ties to Russia would make it difficult for the Central Asian governments to create independent economies after 1991. The decade of the 1990s saw serious economic disruption and widespread hardship, while a few people became rich, and the presidents consolidated and expanded their power. The economic situation changed dramatically after the turn of the century as the price of oil and gas and of gold, copper, and other minerals produced in Central Asia soared. New pipelines and other infrastructure were constructed to service the export boom and the value of output rose rapidly, especially in the energy exporters Kazakhstan and Turkmenistan. For the poorer countries, Tajikistan and the Kyrgyz Republic, the demand for migrant workers provided a new connection to Russia. After the resource boom ended in 2015, the Central Asian countries searched for ways to diversify their economies away from dependence on resource exports and remittances. Creating non-resource exports was seen to be the most promising strategy and this required improved infrastructure oriented towards new markets and regional cooperation among the landlocked countries. Section 3 describes these three episodes in Central Asia's post-independence economic history.

The search for economic and political independence dominated the three decades after 1991, albeit as autocratic leaders raised in the Soviet Union had some ambivalence about market mechanisms and globalization. After 2016, a new generation of Central Asian leaders came to power, for whom the centrally planned economy was a more distant memory and other neighbours and partners were as important as Russia. Section 4 connects the economic developments to the desire for more diversified foreign relations, referred to in the region as multi-vector foreign policies. The United States became an important player after 2001 due to its involvement in Afghanistan, but more important in the long term was the growth of trade with China and with the EU and the development of east-west transport links between these two partners. The process has been accelerated by Russia's invasion of Ukraine and the search for east-west Eurasian rail links that avoid Russia.

This Element is being written during the second year of the war in Ukraine, whose outcome is uncertain and will surely impact on the strength of relations between Russia and Central Asia. Russia will remain an important partner and influence on Central Asia. Nevertheless, the pattern of strengthening relations with other partners will surely continue and the special relationship with Russia will become less special. Kazakhstan is by geography and history likely to remain most connected to Russia but embracement of the C5+1 format indicates that Kazakhstan sees its future as a Central Asian country rather than part of the Russian sphere.

2 Incorporation into the Tsarist and Soviet Empires

2.1 Central Asia before the Russian Conquest

The heartland of Central Asia is the basin formed by the two great rivers that flow into the Aral Sea: the Oxus and Jaxartes of ancient history, the Amudarya and Syrdarya in modern times (Map 2). Historically, an important distinction was between the sedentary populations based in the oases and valleys, and the nomadic populations of the steppe. At least from the time of Alexander the Great (who married a Central Asian princess) two and a half thousand years ago, trade routes from the eastern Mediterranean and Mesopotamia to China had been established with way stations at oases and strategic points on the river systems of Central Asia.

Nomadic people from the north frequently disrupted what became later known as the Silk Road in their search for plunder.[6] Control over the region changed over time, with some rulers leaving more lasting impact. Arab armies conquered the region in 751 and brought Islam to Central Asia.[7] When their power crumbled a century later, the Persian Samanid successor state made its capital Bukhara into one of Islam's greatest cultural and scientific centres. The end of Samanid rule in 999 was followed by several centuries of disruption from Turkic invaders, until in the thirteenth century Chinggis Khan united most of Eurasia into the world's largest ever land empire and the Silk Road thrived again. After Chinggis' successors fell

---

[6] Much more than silk was traded along these routes. The *Silk Road* label dates only from the 1870s when it was coined by Ferdinand von Richthofen, uncle of Snoopy's nemesis the Red Baron.

[7] Our intellectual heritage is captured in words like algebra and algorithm. The former is from the title of a book *Kitab al-jabr wa al-muqabalah* written around 825 by Abū ʿAbdallāh Muḥammad ibn Mūsā al-Khwārizmī, whose name indicating that he came from Khwarizm (Khorezm – an oasis shared by modern-day Uzbekistan and Turkmenistan) is loosely transcribed as algorithm.

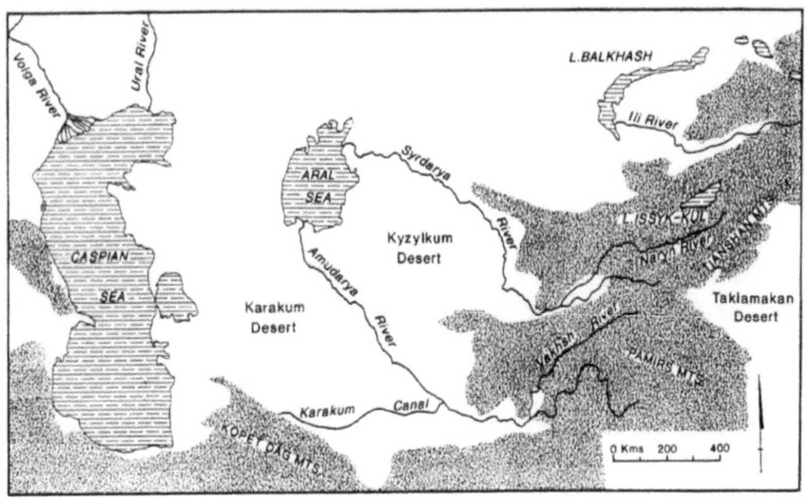

Map 2 The Aral Sea Basin

into dispute and the empire fragmented, the final flourish came at the end of the
fourteenth century when Timur (Tamerlane) created an empire from Egypt to India,
and made his capital, Samarkand, a new centre of Islamic culture and scientific
learning.

The nomadic Uzbeks began to take over the remnants of Tamerlane's empire
in the late fifteenth century. With the discovery of cheaper ocean routes around
1500, the overland Silk Road between Europe and Asia dwindled in significance, and the importance of the formerly great cities of Bukhara, Samarkand,
and Kashgar diminished. Central Asia was ruled by a kaleidoscope of local
rulers in cities whose territories grew and declined, although much of the region
was outside their control, especially in the south-west where Turkmen clans
dominated. Other nomadic peoples such as the Kazakhs, Kyrgyz, Karakalpaks,
and Mongols lived further north. Their horsemen sometimes conquered large
areas but failed to establish the administrative structure to maintain a large
empire (or did so only by losing their nomadic character, as in the case of Kublai
Khan in China). Changes in military technology permanently ended the threat
of nomadic hordes sweeping through rich settled areas; in the late seventeenth
and early eighteenth centuries Xinjiang, Mongolia, and Tibet were brought
under Chinese rule, and most of the Kazakh clans accepted Russian protection.

The correspondence between economic basis and cultural characteristics was
close in some respects. The nomads were primarily Turkic/Mongol-speaking
groups, and their political organization bore little relation to the modern state;
local strongmen ruled on the basis of clan loyalties and a feudal system of
vassalage. The cities were home to Persian-speaking Tajiks, Han Chinese, and

more recently Russians. In practice, ethnic groups often intermixed, obscuring clear-cut ethnic boundaries.

In the early nineteenth century, Central Asia was dominated by three rulers – the Emir of Bukhara, the Khan of Kokand, and the Khan of Khiva – who exercised despotic rule over their domains. Although military technology had long ago made their defences inadequate against modern artillery, they were protected by mountains from the military might of Britain to the south and by deserts from the growing power of Russia to the north. Tsarist Russia had been preoccupied since the 1550s with extending its empire east to the Pacific (including taking most of the Kazakhs under their protection) and south through the Caucasus.

2.2 Conquest and Tsarist Rule

Once Russia and Britain had ended the Napoleonic threat, the two great powers turned their attention to Central Asia. Russian armies had already subdued much of the Caucasus, and by 1813 they reached the Persian Empire and agreed upon a border at the Aras River. Central Asia was the obvious next acquisition. The British had no ambition to extend their Empire into Central Asia, but they feared the Russian advance and suspected that the Tsar's goal was India. The first step for both sides was to explore the region and establish which deserts were impassable and which mountain passes impregnable, and which local despots could be bought. The missions by Nikolai Muraviev to Khiva in 1819 and by William Moorcroft, George Trebeck, and George Guthrie to Bukhara in 1820 were the opening moves in what became known in both English and Russian as the Great Game (or *Bolshaya igra*).

The emirates of Central Asia were no match militarily for Russian armies, and their only natural defences were the huge deserts which had foiled early Russian moves against Central Asia. In 1717, a Russian expedition of 4,000 men marched to Khiva, only to arrive exhausted and be slaughtered, with just some forty survivors. Once the Russians had overcome the logistical problems of getting troops and their equipment into Central Asia in good shape, then military victory would be easy. This they did gradually, culminating in the complete subjugation of the region after the construction of railways in the 1880s.

Initial Russian moves were unsuccessful. In 1838, an attack by Russia's ally Persia on the strategic city of Herat in Afghanistan was repulsed by Afghan forces with British help, and the Shah of Persia withdrew in the face of British threats in the Gulf. Britain followed up by establishing a puppet regime in Afghanistan, supported by a large British garrison. In response, Russia sent a force of 5,000 men from Orenburg to take Khiva but devastated by a harsh winter the troops turned back after three months, losing 1,000 men without engaging the enemy. Nemesis for Britain quickly followed when demonstrations in Kabul in the winter of 1841–2 forced the British garrison to withdraw; of 16,000 people who set out through the Khyber Pass only one made it to the safety of Jalalabad, completing one of the British Empire's worst ever military disasters.[8] A decade of Anglo-Russian detente followed these mutual disasters in Central Asia, until events elsewhere and botched diplomacy triggered the 1853–6 Crimean War.

The Great Game revived after the 1860 Treaty of Peking allowed Russia to consolidate its far eastern possessions and to open consulates in Urga (modern Ulaanbaatar) and Kashgar (Kashi). The US Civil War directed attention to Central Asia, as disruption of the main source of cotton increased the attractiveness of annexing the Kokand region, which contained the Fergana Valley known to be suitable for cotton-growing. After annexing the small oasis towns of Chimkent and Turkestan in the northern part of the Kokand khanate in 1864, in the following year 1,900 Russian soldiers with twelve artillery guns defeated a defending force of 30,000 to capture Tashkent, the largest town in Central Asia (Map 3).

General Konstantin von Kaufman was appointed Governor-General of Tashkent, and from there he oversaw the Russian conquest of Central Asia. In 1868 Samarkand was captured, and the Emir of Bukhara accepted a treaty making him a Russian vassal. In late 1869, the Russians began construction of a fort at Krasnovodsk on the eastern shore of the Caspian Sea (today's Turkmenbashi port). The fort provided one base for a three-pronged attack on Khiva in 1873, with two other forces coming from Tashkent and Orenburg. This time the Russian troops reached Khiva, and after a few artilleries rounds the defenders fled. The khanate became a Russian protectorate, which von Kaufman integrated into the empire in 1875. Meanwhile, at the other end of Central Asia, an Islamic uprising had led to the establishment of an independent state centred on Kashgar, and the Russians took advantage of the situation to annex Ili in northern Xinjiang in 1871. Thus, in about a decade, the Russian Empire had incorporated most of Central Asia, coming to within 200 miles of British India and eating into Chinese Turkestan (Map 3).

During the second half of the 1870s, both Britain and China responded more actively. Britain mobilized diplomatically to ensure that Russia gained little from a 1877–8 war with Turkey, and then punished the Afghan ruler for friendship with Russia by invading and imposing an unequal treaty on Afghanistan. Although British occupation was again unpopular and led to

---

[8] Symbolic of the British decline was the public beheading in 1842 of two British agents in Bukhara, whose emir clearly no longer feared retribution. Peter Hopkirk's 1990 book on the Great Game captures the swashbuckling nature of the contest.

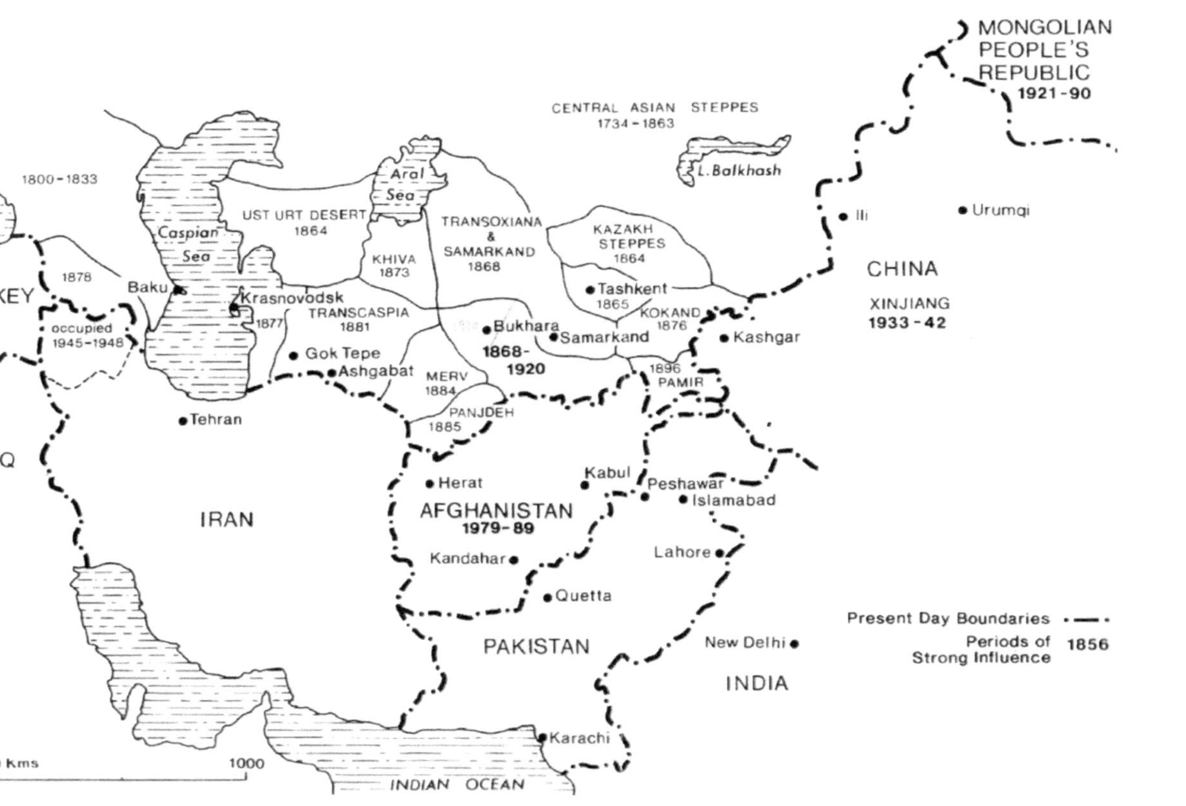

Map 3 Expansion of the Russian Empire in Central Asia

another military defeat during the withdrawal, the Second Afghan War ended successfully insofar as Britain established a strong ruler over a unified Afghan state who remained within the British sphere of influence for the remainder of the Great Game. China put down the rebellion and recaptured Kashgar in 1878, thwarting Russian ambitions to eventually take the town. The 1881 Treaty of St. Petersburg established the Russo-Chinese border in Central Asia, returning Ili to Chinese rule; Russian hawks criticized the treaty as a climbdown, but since 1949 China has denounced it as an unequal treaty imposed on China.

The final Russian advance came against the Turkmen. In 1879, a Russian attack on the stronghold of Gök Tepe had failed when the commander overconfidently resorted to an infantry attack rather than relying on superior firepower. In 1881, a second attack succeeded when artillery and sappers destroyed the defences, after which defending soldiers and civilians were massacred. The Transcaspian railway, begun in Krasnovodsk in 1880 followed the military advance. In 1884 the Turkmen capital, Merv (Mary), submitted to Russian rule, and the railway reached Merv the following year. By 1888 the railway reached Samarkand. The Russian army moved south towards Herat but threatened by war with Britain halted at the oasis of Pandjeh. A border commission established Russia's southern international boundary, which was not crossed until 1979.

The last episode in the Great Game took place in the high Pamir Mountains in the 1890s. Russia claimed the Pamirs region, but Britain resisted this advance by conquering or reducing to dependence the local fiefdoms and thus plugging the last holes in India's northern defences. After the turn of the century, the Great Game between Russia and Britain wound down. In 1903–4 a British force invaded Tibet, convinced they would uncover evidence of Russian plotting in Lhasa, but found nothing and retired. Meanwhile, in 1904–5 Russia was unexpectedly defeated by Japan, reinforcing the view in Britain that Germany was now the real rival. Russia had its internal problems too with the 1905 abortive revolution. The 1907 Anglo-Russian Convention formalized the end of the Great Game, establishing frontiers and spheres of influence.

The converging of the Russian, Persian, British, and Chinese empires by the beginning of the twentieth century established international boundaries. The only area of Central Asia to escape conquest was Afghanistan, but it was included in the line-drawing as a narrow strip of land running to China's border, the Wakhan Corridor, was declared Afghan territory to prevent the contiguity of the Russian and British empires. The old international borders remained in place even after the disintegration of the USSR.[9]

---

[9] Xinjiang, although under Chinese rule, was practically independent from 1912 to 1931 when it became 'a nominally Chinese province under Soviet protection' (Nyman, 1977, 130). In November 1933, a Turkic Islamic Republic of East Turkestan was established in Kashgar but it

Although incorporation of Central Asia into the Russian Empire had a lasting impact on international borders, the domestic impact was limited. Central Asia was mostly ruled by a governor-general based in Tashkent whose principal task was to maintain Russian power. Although the military government had vast powers in principle, implementation was constrained by large distances and small numbers of staff (Mankoff, 2022; Morrison, 2012). The Russian authorities applied a soft touch to Central Asian institutions and customs. Islamic law continued to be applied and education was outside state control. The Emir of Bukhara and the Khan of Khiva continued to rule, albeit as Russian vassals; the Khan of Kokand was deposed in 1876 after an anti-Russian revolt on his territory.

The rulers, like European imperialists elsewhere, saw themselves as having a civilizing mission, but assumed that would be achieved by example rather than imposition. In the cities, the Russian and other immigrants lived in a new modern city while the old Central Asian city was left alone; the native population were expected to see the benefits of modern civilization and abandon the unhygienic squalor of their traditional housing. In rural areas, colonists would demonstrate the benefits of modern farming.[10]

The half-century of Russian rule was not without changes in Central Asian society. In the early twentieth century a group started to press for modernizing reform of the Islamic communities, but the Jadidists' impact was slight. In the areas that had been controlled by Bukhara, Kokand and Khiva, traditional norms remained strong, especially with respect to the roles of women and of religious leaders.

The main economic interest lay in developing the cotton belt through the irrigable lands of the Ferghana Valley and the region between the two major rivers. Railway lines connecting Tashkent to the Caspian Sea and from Tashkent to Orenburg (and Moscow) had military and economic purposes. Railway workers were a significant component of the working class, especially in Tashkent. Banks and other financial institutions were primarily involved in supporting construction and cotton. Some farmers migrated from other parts

---

was suppressed in 1934. An attempt by the Chinese government to re-establish control over Xinjiang in 1944 led to an uprising and declaration in 1945 of the Eastern Turkestan Republic. There is debate over whether the 1944/5 Eastern Turkestan uprising was fomented by the USSR (the official Chinese view at the time) or whether it was a nationalist response to autocratic and oppressive Chinese rule (Benson, 1990). Only after the suppression of the uprising in 1949/50 did Xinjiang come effectively under the control of the central government of China. The 1953 population of 4.9 million included 3.6 million Uygurs and few Han Chinese, but by the 1980s the 6 million Uygurs accounted for less than half of Xinjiang 's population.

[10] The sense of European superiority was strong. The claim to be modernizing agriculture was ironic, given that emancipation of serfs in Russia was as recent as 1861. Paul Stronski (2010, 16–29) describes the 'Russian Model' for pre-Soviet Tashkent.

of the Russian Empire to Central Asia, leading to conflicts with the native population over land.[11] Otherwise, the impact of Russian rule on most of the Central Asian population was limited.

The great nineteenth-century empires ruled from Constantinople, Vienna, and Moscow were multicultural, and their collapse after World War I would lead to subdivision. Dividing the spoils looked set to be a messy business in all cases. Surprisingly, the collapse of the Tsarist regime in 1917 and the establishment of the Soviet Union had no impact on international boundaries in Central Asia. The Bolsheviks tore up Russia's treaties and Anglo-Russian confrontation revived in the Caucasus and Central Asia. British troops intervened in Baku and Ashgabat; British politicians (among the most vocal was Winston Churchill), who argued for taking advantage of the widespread internal opposition to communist rule to push back the frontiers of the Soviet empire, lost the debate and British troops withdrew.

2.3 Revolt and Revolution

Central Asian revolts in 1916–26 were triggered by resistance to conscription of previously exempt Muslims, were maintained by opposition to settlers and by rural–urban conflicts, and were fuelled in turn by colonial violence of Slavs and Cossacks who had moved into the region since the 1860s. Although opposition to conscription was the trigger, the 25 June 1916 decree to mobilize labourers for the war effort was issued also to indigenous peoples of other parts of the Russian Empire (Siberia, the Caucasus and Kalmykia) without the same violent reaction. The causes of revolt had built up in Central Asia over decades of Russian rule, and opposition to non-indigenous groups and violent retaliation by those groups played a part. Protests were violently repressed both by the Tsarist authorities in 1916 and by Soviet authorities after 1917.

The February and October revolutions in St. Petersburg in 1917 had echoes in Central Asia. Russian workers in railway centres, notably Tashkent, were in favour of the Bolshevik revolution and on 30 April 1918 they proclaimed the Turkestan Autonomous Soviet Socialist Republic (ASSR), an autonomous republic of the Russian Soviet Federative Socialist Republic covering the southern part of Kazakhstan and the territory of the other four modern Central Asian countries. The Tashkent Soviet was an organization of workers and had few Central Asian members – in contrast to the ideology of the central government which saw Communism as a universal system applying equally to all races. A regime based on the dictatorship of the proletariat faced problems adapting to a region without

---

[11] Daniel Brower (2003) argues that the inflow of settlers in the early 1900s, encouraged by authorities in Saint Petersburg, was the major destabilizing factor behind the protests of 1916.

an indigenous proletariat and, although the Turkestan ASSR had support of modernizing groups in the Central Asian population such as the Young Bukharans, the number of Central Asians actively involved was small.[12]

After the Bolsheviks assumed power, Central Asia was cut off from Moscow by anti-Communist forces. An Orenburg Cossack fragment of the White counterrevolutionary armies regained Orenburg in November 1918, allowing them to disrupt the railway between Russia and Tashkent. The Red Army broke the Cossack resistance in November 1919 and re-established the Moscow-Tashkent rail link. Events in Central Asia were confusing and driven as much by famine as by political agendas; between 1915 and 1920, war and famine led to hundreds of thousands of deaths, and many more became refugees.[13]

The crucial battles and campaigns during the civil wars following the revolutions of 1917 were elsewhere.[14] The main battlefield in Central Asia was the Transcaspian front, where the Turkestan ASSR faced an anti-Bolshevik uprising in July 1918. Troops from Tashkent entered Ashkhabad in July 1919 and pushed their opponents across the Caspian Sea in February 2020. The capture of the Caspian port of Krasnovodsk (Turkmenbashi today) by Soviet troops in February 1920, the month when the main White armies collapsed in the rest of the Soviet Union, signalled the end of serious rebellion in Central Asia as the Soviet authorities controlled the rail network. The Khan of Khiva and Emir of Bukhara, who had retained nominal independence in the Tsarist Empire, were ejected in 1920 and replaced by Soviet republics in their territories. In rural areas, the Basmachi, who largely consisted of loosely organized self-defence groups against settlers, were the major source of anti-Soviet resistance. They continued to operate throughout the 1920s without threatening Soviet rule, in part due to internal disputes between ultra-conservatives and liberal Jadidists who had become disillusioned with Soviet rule and between groups of different ethnic origins.[15]

Some of the events in 1917–20 could be seen as the first shoots of Central Asian national consciousness. The Jadidist reformers looked to create a modernizing regime, with similarities to the Turkish government that emerged from the ashes

---

[12] Opposition episodes like the Osipov internal uprising in January 1919 or resistance by an anti-Bolshevik regime in Kokand also involved no more than a few thousand participants.

[13] Adeeb Khalid (2021, 161) reports estimates that 39 per cent of the sedentary Muslim population and 46 per cent of Central Asian nomads died between 1915 and 1920.

[14] Jonathan Smele (2015) argues that, although the 1916 Central Asian protests were the opening shots of civil wars on the territory of the Tsarist Empire and the ongoing Basmachi activities after 1926 the last lingering elements of those wars, Central Asia was a sideshow to the main actions in the Russian Soviet Republic and in Ukraine and the western fringes of the empire.

[15] Jonathan Smele (2015, 235) refers to 'bitter hostilities … especially between Turkmens and Uzbeks and Kirghiz and Uzbeks'. He argues that the revolt was 'nearing its demise' after the summer of 1922 even though guerrilla groups operated from the mountains or across the border with Afghanistan until 1931 or 1934 or possibly 1938.

of the Ottoman Empire, but they lacked wider support – as well as facing implacable opposition from the traditional religious leaders.[16] The Soviet authorities helped. Officials brought settlers to justice for atrocities committed against Central Asian peoples in 1916–17, and many were forcibly returned to Russia. The Bolshevik Party also promoted gender equality, granting women the vote in 1917 and encouraging opposition to dress codes and other practices supported by the conservative religious leadership.

Within the Bolshevik Party, there was active discussion of the nationalities issue that was seen to have undermined the Austro-Hungarian Empire. The debate was resolved by mid-1923 in favour of what Terry Martin (2001) has labelled Affirmative Action on nationalities within the Soviet empire. A new constitution in 1922 defined the Soviet Union as a federal state based on national territorial autonomy. The political map was redrawn to acknowledge not only the dozen full Soviet republics but also hundreds of national territories within those republics. In Central Asia, Bukhara and Khiva disappeared as separate entities, and the borders of the new republics drawn up in 1924 would, with changes over the next twelve years, form the borders of the new independent states in December 1991.

The most successful nation-building was in the Turkmen Republic (Edgar, 2004). Elites from a loose association of tribes who based legitimacy on genealogy learned to adapt to the Soviet nationality definition, welcoming creation of a common Turkmen language and flag. At the same time, the elites opposed modernization, especially agrarian reform to transform nomads into cotton farmers. The process was a success in that in 1991 Turkmenistan was the most ethnically homogenous of the new independent countries (Table 1), and the elements of Soviet nationality policy carried through, with emphasis on the national language (written in Latin script after 1993 to emphasize the downgrading of Russian) and on the national homeland within the Soviet republic's borders, downplaying the nomadic heritage (with some contradiction to the ongoing respect for equestrian skill). Central planning was replaced less by a market-based economy than by a revival of traditional economic relationships based on Islam or other customary law and an autocratic leader.

The significance of the national-based entities in Central Asia was underlined by the 1923 indigenization (*korenziatsiia*) program that encouraged school teaching in native languages and preference for indigenous peoples in the workplace. However, all decision-making powers remained centralized in Moscow. Exercise of those central powers could promote new attitudes; Cameron (2018) argues that the collectivization and sedentarization of agriculture in Kazakhstan after the

---

[16] The government of a People's Soviet Republic of Bukhara from August 2020 to May 2023 was dominated by modernizing Jadidists, but they were brought into line by Moscow and the leaders were exiled.

Table 1 Population of the five Central Asian republics in 1989, in thousands

	Soviet Republic				
	Kazakh	**Kyrgyz**	**Tajik**	**Turkmen**	**Uzbek**
Kazakh	6,535	37	11	88	808
Kyrgyz	14	2,230	64	1	175
Tajik	25	34	3,172	3	934
Turkmen	4	1	20	2,537	122
Uzbek	332	550	1,198	317	14,142
Russian	6,228	917	388	334	1,653
Ukrainian	896	108	41	36	153
Belorussian	183	9	7	9	29
German	958	101	33	4	40
Tartar	328	70	72	39	657
Karakalpak	–	–	–	–	412
Korean	103	18	13	–	183
Uigur	185	37	–	–	36
Total	**16,563**	**4,290**	**5,109**	**3,534**	**19,905**

Source: Pomfret (1995, 5), data from the 1989 Soviet census.

famine of the early 1930s contributed to creation of a Soviet identity among the survivors and of a Kazakh identity that had not previously existed.[17]

In practice, the region was pacified by 1926, just in time for the implementation of Soviet modernization. On International Women's Day, 9 March 1927, the campaign for Central Asian women to cast off the veil was inaugurated, and strongly opposed by many Central Asian men.[18] This soon merged into a wider campaign against religion in the Soviet Union, which included abolition of Islamic courts and closure of madrasas. During the 1930s, Central Asians became more prominent in authority, but typically of a younger generation; the older Jadidists were decried as bourgeois reformers, and many were killed after show trials in 1937–8. By 1941, Soviet citizenship had been accepted and many Central Asians fought in the Great Patriotic War, in stark contrast to the anti-conscription riots of 1916. At the same time, the creation of separate republics also fostered pride in Central Asian heritage.

---

[17] In her introduction to a book forum on Cameron (2018) in the *Journal of Genocide Research 23(4)* 2021, Sarah Cameron says on page 161 'Nomadism, not nationality, was the defining feature of Kazakh identity prior to the famine'.

[18] Several authors (e.g. Douglas Northrop and Marianne Kamp) have assessed this and similar programs as failures. However, even if religious practices continued to contribute to subjugation of women, there can be little doubt that women fared better in Soviet Central Asia than in more traditional Islamic societies to the south.

2.4 Central Asia in the Centrally Planned Economy

At least in the early decades of the Soviet Union, the perception among the Soviet leadership was that the USSR was the cutting edge of what would become a global revolution, and Central Asia would be a model for poorer countries. Social policies were a major improvement over the casual neglect of the Tsarist regime. Education and health services succeeded in raising literacy and life expectancy in Central Asia to close to First World levels.

Despite these undisputed benefits, there is ongoing debate over whether the benefits were outweighed by a colonial status that led to Central Asia being exploited for its wealth of cotton and minerals.[19] Central Asia's role in the Soviet division of labour was as supplier of raw materials: cotton for Russian mills, coal and metals for Russia's industries, natural gas to heat Russian homes and power Russian factories, and so on. Roads and railways went north to Russia, rather than connecting places within Central Asia; the south-north pattern already established in the Tsarist Empire was reinforced by completion in 1930 of the Turksib railway linking Tashkent to Siberia through Kazakhstan. Pipelines took Central Asian natural gas and oil north to Russia, while electricity and gas grids were designed in Moscow without concern for republics' borders. Central Asia's southern borders with Iran and Afghanistan and eastern border with China were sealed, apart from a conduit through Termez in southern Uzbekistan for military supplies after the 1979 invasion of Afghanistan.

The hope that Turkestan's cotton would absolve the empire of the need to import cotton was present in the Tsarist empire (Obertreis, 2017) but the Bolsheviks turned 'cotton independence' into the main obligation of Uzbekistan and Turkmenistan. Grandiose projects of transforming nature and making the desert bloom were dreamed up in the Tsarist period, but it was Soviet planners who implemented many of these grand projects, especially in the stable years after World War II. The Hungry Steppe was irrigated and the Karakum Canal was built.[20] Greater investment and provision of technical support for 'engineerization', 'chemicalization,' and 'mechanization' were intended to remove limits set by nature. Cotton production targets kept increasing; Uzbekistan had produced 515,000 tons in 1928, but by

---

[19] The net resource transfers are impossible to quantify because a large part of the transfers were physical movements within all-union enterprises, whose value by any monetary metric was unknown. Similarly, the transfer of health, education, and other social services to Central Asia was not given a monetary value. Michaels (2003) argues that building a scientific medical system in Kazakhstan was primarily aimed at transferring allegiances from old authorities (mullahs, shamans) to new Soviet authorities, but it still brought substantial public health benefits.

[20] Excavation of the Karakum Canal, diverting water from the Amu Darya River through southern Turkmenistan, began in 1954 and by 1988 it was 1,375 kilometres long. The canal opened up new land for agriculture, primarily cotton, and supplied water to the Turkmen capital, Ashgabat. It was also the principal contributor to the desiccation of the Aral Sea.

the 1980s Uzbek farmers were being exhorted to reach annual production of six million tons. The Turkmen and Tajik republics, and to a much lesser extent the Kyrgyz republic and Kazakhstan were also expected to contribute to Soviet cotton production.

There were variations in the republics' economies. Following the German invasion in 1941, factories were relocated from the western USSR to Siberia and Central Asia. Tashkent became a manufacturing centre, cementing its position as the largest Central Asian city (and fifth largest in the USSR).[21] Kazakhstan's economy became more diverse as mining became important, especially in the coal and iron complex at Karaganda but also in some thirty 'company towns' that typically developed around a mine or smelter. Between 1954 and 1964, the 'Virgin Lands' of northern Kazakhstan became an important area of grain cultivation with c.20 million hectares of new land brought into production, populated by 650,000 virgin-landers, mainly farmers from Slavic Soviet republics.[22] In the final decade of the Soviet Union, natural gas fields were developed in Turkmenistan and, in the largest foreign investment deal in Soviet history, Chevron committed in 1990 to develop the Tengiz oilfield in northwest Kazakhstan. In the two poorest republics, Soviet planners connected projects for regional development to foreign commitments; the largest factory in the Kyrgyz republic refined cane sugar from Cuba, and in the South Tajikistan Territorial Complex bauxite from Guinea was smelted into aluminium using hydroelectric power.

The image of happy Central Asian workers was belied by occasional signs of dissent in the major cities.[23] In 1966 after a major earthquake shook Tashkent, workers from across the Soviet Union joined in the rebuilding of a modern city. Amidst the official reports of fraternal gratitude, there were also incidents of Uzbek youths exhorting Russians to go home. The Tashkent football club, Pakhtakor, became a focal source of Uzbek pride. After the Uzbek First Secretary, Sharof Rashidov, was targeted in the anti-corruption drive of Yuri Andropov (USSR General Secretary 1982–4) for massive over-invoicing of Uzbek cotton deliveries to Russia, he became an Uzbek national hero; Rashidov

---

[21] Over one hundred factories and 150,000 skilled workers were relocated to Uzbekistan during the war. Some moved back to their original locations after 1943 but some industries remained in Tashkent, for example, aircraft production.

[22] In 1961, the railway junction Akmolinsk was renamed Tselinograd (City of the Virgin Lands); in 1997, it would become the capital of Kazakhstan, known first as Akmola and later renamed Astana. Cities along the Itrtysh River in north-eastern Kazakhstan were also populated by non-Kazakhs. The Baikonur Cosmodrome in Central Kazakhstan was the Soviet space centre, from which Yuri Gagarin became the first man to orbit the earth.

[23] There were also environmental concerns connected especially to the desiccation of the Aral Sea, the world's fourth largest lake in the early Soviet era, and to open-air nuclear testing in north-eastern Kazakhstan.

avoided punishment by his timely death in 1983, and after 1991 a main street in Tashkent was renamed in his honour.

The practice in the non-Russian republics of having a First Secretary from the titular nationality and a Russian Second Secretary was widely seen as evidence of Russian control over the Soviet empire.[24] When Moscow deviated from this practice in Kazakhstan in 1986 by replacing Dinmukhamed Kunaev as First Secretary by a Russian, demonstrations in the capital city Alma-Ata (Almaty after independence) were violently suppressed and an unknown number of demonstrators killed. Again, the Central Asian leader who was charged with corruption would be rehabilitated after 1991. The martyrs of 1986 are now honoured by a prominent monument.

In sum, there were signs of national consciousness in the Central Asian Soviet republics, but protests were limited, whether by fear of repression or due to satisfaction with improved living standards. In 1989, the republics declared the titular language to be the official language and in 1990 they made declarations of autonomy, that is, assertion of republican sovereignty over natural resources; these moves were following the lead of other Soviet republics, including Russia. In the April 1991 referendum on the future of the Soviet Union, the Central Asian republics voted overwhelmingly in support of continuation of the Union and there were no demonstrations comparable to events in the Baltic republics, the Ukraine republic, or even parts of the Russian republic. After the failure of the attempted coup by hardliners in Moscow in August 1991, the end came quickly.[25] When the USSR was dissolved on 25 December 1991, the Central Asian republics were the least prepared for independence.

2.5 Dissolution of the Soviet Union

In December 1991, Russia's President Boris Yeltsin willingly acquiesced to the independence of the Central Asian republics. Kazakhstan's leader Nursultan Nazarbayev was particularly close to Yeltsin and an important figure in trying to maintain links among the former Soviet republics. As one of the inheritors of the Soviet nuclear arsenal, Kazakhstan received treaty commitments guaranteeing the new country's territorial integrity in return for collaboration in decommissioning Kazakhstan's nuclear weapons. Russia supported the successor states' accession to the United Nations in 1992 and during the 1990s Russia's government appeared to

---

[24] Russians also occupied the power positions of chairman of the KGB in each republic and of Commander of the Turkestan Military District.

[25] The Uzbek and Kyrgyz republics declared independence on August 31, the Tajik republic on September 7, the Turkmen republic in October and Kazakhstan in December, but these statements had little meaning and international recognition of independence only came after December 25.

have no irredentist designs, although respect for the territorial integrity of the new UN members was not universal in Russia. President Yeltsin was more concerned about holding the Russian Federation together as the economy suffered severe transitional recession and as he increased democracy, for example, with elected regional governors.

The Central Asian successor states' response to dissolution of the USSR was not uniform. In all five countries, leaders focused on nation-building and cementing their personal power, while overseeing economic transition from central planning to a market-based system. Uzbekistan sought to become a close US ally and Turkmenistan obtained a UN Declaration of Neutrality in 1995, while both countries adopted a cautious approach to economic reform. Kazakhstan and especially Kyrgyzstan were more ambitious in economic reform, and more anxious to maintain links with Russia. Tajikistan was the only Central Asian country not to have a peaceful passage to independence; civil war between 1992 and 1997 claimed between 50,000 and 100,000 lives. By 1999, all five countries had presidential regimes and varieties of market-based economies. Economic links to Russia declined as the Yeltsin government faced economic difficulties (highlighted by debt default in 1998) and political problems (highlighted by war in Chechnya), and the Central Asian countries found new export markets.

The United States and EU member countries opened embassies, but during the 1990s the West showed little interest in Central Asia. September 2001 was a turning point in US interest, primarily due to the War on Terror and need for bases to supply troops in Afghanistan. The United States rented airbases in Uzbekistan until 2005 and in the Kyrgyz Republic until 2014 through which most troops passed and organized a northern distribution network of overland freight transport from Baltic ports to Afghanistan.

The Commonwealth of Independent States (CIS) was intended to maintain continuity of relations between the non-Baltic former Soviet republics, but support was lukewarm. Turkmenistan preferred to emphasize its neutrality, which was recognized in a 1995 UN Resolution, and other successor states split between the GUAM (Georgia, Ukraine, Azerbaijan, and Moldova) grouping and the Union of Five (Russia, Belarus, Kazakhstan, the Kyrgyz Republic, and Tajikistan – later the Eurasian Economic Community).

Uzbekistan allied with the United States in 1996–7, occasionally being together with Israel the only countries voting with the United States in the UN General Assembly, and aligned with the GUAM group, which was briefly called GUUAM. The May 2005 Andijan events, when Uzbek troops dispersed a demonstration by killing hundreds of unarmed people, disrupted relations with the West. Uzbekistan joined the Russian-led Eurasian Economic Community between 2005 and 2008. The Shanghai Cooperation Organization seemed to become more attractive than the West for autocrats, but in 2005–8 there was little evidence of increased Russian influence in Central Asia. In 2008, the Central Asian countries did not recognize Abkhazia or South Ossetia – and the Shanghai Cooperation Organization with China appeared to be a counterweight to Russia rather than a conduit for Russian influence. In 2008, Uzbekistan quit the Eurasian Economic Community.

After 2009 Russia reasserted its influence, focussing on links to willing partners rather than attempting to control the entire former Soviet space. The customs union with Kazakhstan and Belarus was not a new initiative, but after 2010 implementation became effective. The customs union was extended in 2015 as the Eurasian Economic Union (EAEU) with aspirations to deeper economic integration and with Armenia and the Kyrgyz Republic as additional members.

The revival of Russian influence can be ascribed to Putin's nostalgia for the USSR and Greater Russia, but it also reflected changing economic circumstances. The 1999–2015 resource boom allowed Russia to pay off its debts in the first half of the 2000s and increasingly to modernize and upgrade its military. The most direct impact on Central Asia of Russia's resource boom was the rapid increase in employment of migrant workers from Central Asia in Russia to the extent that Tajikistan and the Kyrgyz Republic became the world's most remittance-dependent countries in 2014.[26] Threats of changes to migrants' status gave Russia influence; the position of migrants, plus promised financial aid, were the principal carrots offered for EAEU accession and accepted by the Kyrgyz Republic but not by Tajikistan.

Nevertheless, the long-term trend has been of reduced Russian economic influence. The Central Asian countries found new markets for their exports and new suppliers of imports and joined new value chains. The changing trade patterns were reinforced by new infrastructure – especially pipelines and railways – that led to the east and to the west rather than to the north, reducing dependence on Russia. These developments will be analysed in Sections 3 and 4.

2.6 Where Are the Boundaries in and of Central Asia?

The incorporation of Central Asia into the Russian Empire and then the Soviet Union had a determining impact on actual present-day borders. However, there may be doubts about physical or ethnic borders. To the west Central Asia is

---

[26] Booming resource exports strengthened the value of the Russian ruble, making Russia's other traded goods uncompetitive and shifting consumption towards non-traded goods and services such as construction, where unskilled labour was needed for jobs that Russian men were unwilling to do for the wages paid to Central Asian workers. The remittances to GDP ratio was 42 per cent in Tajikistan and 30 per cent in the Kyrgyz Republic in 2014, when four or five million Central Asians worked at least part of the year in Russia. The value of remittances fell in 2015 as the oil boom ended and the Russian ruble's value dropped.

bordered by the Caspian Sea and to the east some of the world's highest mountains divide Central Asia from China. The Köpet Dag hills dividing Turkmenistan from Iran and the river border between Central Asia and Afghanistan have become uncontested historical frontiers. More problematic is the 7,644-kilometre northern border between Kazakhstan and Russian Siberia.

Under Russian imperial rule, most of Central Asia was organized under a Governor General of Turkestan. Some opponents to Soviet rule after 1917 aimed to establish an independent Turkestan and in 1944–9, in the northern part of what is now the Xinjiang Autonomous Region of China, secessionists established the Soviet Republic of East Turkestan, but the prospect of a wide-ranging Turkestan state has held little attraction. Indeed, a first order of business after 1991 was delimitation of the border of China with Kazakhstan, Kyrgyzstan, Tajikistan, and Russia, which had never been precisely determined between the Soviet Union and the People's Republic of China. Issues were resolved amicably among the five countries and the negotiating forum transformed into the Shanghai Cooperation Organization, which Uzbekistan joined in 2001.[27]

In the USSR, Central Asia was divided into separate ethnically based republics, with several border and name readjustments in the 1920s and 1930s. The republic borders became the borders of the new independent states in December 1991. While there is debate over the extent to which the individual republics accurately captured differing compositions of the population, throughout the Soviet era the titular nationality had a majority in the four southern republics. This was documented in the final census of the Soviet Union in 1989 (Table 1). Kazakhstan was the exception with a 1989 population roughly two-fifths Kazakh, two-fifths Russian, and one-fifth other. In Soviet times, the region was often referred to as Central Asia and Kazakhstan.

Kazakh society was pastoral rather than sedentary. The three major Kazakh groupings recognized a common ethnicity, but conflicts were endemic among nomads who fought over grazing rights, and weaker groups would often seek Russian aid, to the extent that Russia gradually imposed a hold over the region (Map 3). Nevertheless, there were strong links, especially to Kyrgyz nomads, and in terms of language and religion also to other Turkic groups in Central Asia.

Kazakhstan had a distinctive history in the first decades of Soviet rule. The 1930–3 famine caused the deaths of between 1.5 and 2 million people, or one-third of ethnic Kazakhs, and the migration of over a million refugees to Russia, China, or Central Asia. The proximate cause was Stalin's imposed collectivization and sedentarization of the agricultural population, destroying the nomadic

---

[27] Although there is sympathy in Central Asia for the Uighurs, the Central Asian governments do not comment on the situation in Xinjiang and maintain amicable relations with China.

settlements and way of life. Disputes remain over whether this was genocide, targeted at Kazakhs, or a tragedy, and whether it was systemic (a consequence of the decision to industrialize rapidly and need to produce grain to feed the industrial workers) or deliberate targeting of Kazakhs.[28] There is no doubt that opposition was ruthlessly crushed, but there is dispute over whether popular opposition and the opposition of rich pastoralists were treated equally. Even after independence, the Kazakh leadership was cautious about opening this can of worms for fear of alienating the large Russian population or even encouraging Russian revanchism, and only in 2020 did President Tokayev create a state commission for rehabilitating the victims of past repression, with the understanding that victims included rich and poor pastoralists.

After the famine, Kazakhs were no longer a majority in the republic. During World War II, Stalin moved millions of people considered security risks from border areas of the USSR to Central Asia; in 1989 there were almost a million Germans, over three hundred thousand Tatars, and a hundred thousand Koreans in Kazakhstan (Table 1). Kazakhstan was also part of the gulag to which political undesirables were assigned (Trotsky is Almaty's most famous resident – Lenin never set foot in Central Asia, despite the ubiquitous statues erected in his honour); Aleksandr Solzhenitsyn's semi-autobiographical novel *Cancer Ward* is set in Kazakhstan and Tashkent.

The Virgin Lands campaign initiated by Khrushchev to make northern Kazakhstan a major grain-growing area led to large-scale immigration of Russians, to the point that they outnumbered Kazakhs in Kazakhstan from the 1960s through the 1980s. Whereas in the other four Central Asian republics, the Russian population was concentrated in the capital city and many left for Russia after 1991, in Kazakhstan a large part of the Russian population was rural and had no wish to leave their homes after 1991. They were concentrated in the north and northeast, close to the Russian border and dependent on Russian rail lines to Black Sea ports for their grain exports.

In the 1993 Russian elections, the Liberal Democratic Party under Vladimir Zhirinovsky, a Russian born in Kazakhstan, whose platform included reincorporation of Kazakhstan into Russia, won 23 per cent of the votes. However, President Nazarbayev was an ally of Yeltsin and knew how to play his cards, relocating the national capital to former Tselinograd, which had been renamed

---

[28] If targeted at Kazakhs, was it the work of the local boss, Filipp Goloshchekin, a Jew to add antisemitism to the brew, or did the buck stop with Joseph Stalin? Cameron (2018) ascribes shared complicity to leading Kazakhs. Wheatcroft (2021), in a critique of Cameron, argues that misperceptions of leaders in Moscow about the agricultural situation in Kazakhstan were the prime cause – top leaders were to blame but it was manslaughter rather than murder. Pianciola (2018) and Kamp and Pianciola (2022) present alternative perspectives on the famine.

Akmola in 1991 and would become Astana in 1998, in the northern (Russified) part of the country and overseeing a readjustment of the population balance while remaining on good terms with Russia. The country welcomed ethnic Kazakhs, primarily from Uzbekistan and from Xinjiang, who were encouraged by higher incomes in Kazakhstan, while most of the large German-origin population flew to Germany and some Russians moved to the Russian Federation.[29]

At the same time, President Nursultan Nazarbayev pursued a multi-vector foreign policy, striving for good relations with China, the United States, the EU, and other partners. His successor, President Kassym-Jomart Tokayev, a career diplomat with experience in China, continued the process. Tokayev also cultivated closer relations with Central Asian leaders and the C5+1 format for the five Central Asian presidents to jointly meet leaders of other countries – sending a signal that independent Kazakhstan is part of Central Asia.

3 Economic Change since 1991

The economic legacy of the Soviet period for Central Asia is disputed. Income levels had risen substantially and social indicators like life expectancy or literacy rates at the end of the Soviet era were high for the income levels (Table 2). By 1990, literacy rates were close to 100 per cent, with only a small percentage of the population, mostly the very old, unable to read and write, in striking contrast to the situation before 1917 or in neighbouring former British colonies.[30] However, even though living standards had improved the Central Asian republics, along with Azerbaijan, had the Soviet Union's highest poverty rates – or, as the Soviet statisticians euphemistically called them, the largest number of under provisioned households.

Central Asian economic history since independence can be divided into three sub-periods.[31] The 1990s were dominated by nation-building and the transition from central planning to market-based economies. From 1999 to 2014, the resource boom especially benefited energy exporters Kazakhstan and Turkmenistan, but also impacted on mineral exports and on the demand

---

[29] Many people of German heritage were able to claim German citizenship and left after the dissolution of the Soviet Union. The first commercial flight from Kazakhstan to outside the CIS was to Hanover.

[30] After reviewing the literature, Obertreis (2017, 146n) concludes that in Turkestan at the beginning of the 1920s 'the literacy rate of indigenous nationalities was no higher than 5%'. In the Turkmen republic before 1917, it is believed that only twenty-five women could read. According to UN statistics, in 1990, 66.2 per cent of Pakistanis and 51.6 per cent of Indians over fifteen had no schooling.

[31] This section draws heavily on my three books (Pomfret, 1995, 2006, 2019) where further details and references can be found.

Table 2 Initial conditions: Republics of the USSR 1989/90

	Population (million) mid−1990	Per capita GNP[a] 1990	Poverty[b] (% of population) 1989	Life expectancy (years) 1990	Literacy rate (% of population) 1990
USSR	289.3	2,870	11.1		
Kazakh	16.8	2,600	15.5	69	97.5
Kyrgyz	4.4	1,570	32.9	68	97.0
Tajik	5.3	1,130	51.2	70	96.7
Turkmen	3.7	1,690	35.0	66	97.7
Uzbek	20.5	1,340	43.6	69	97.2

Source: Pomfret (2006, Table 2.1).

Notes: [a]GNP per capita in US dollars computed by the World Bank's synthetic *Atlas* method.

[b]Individuals in households with gross per capita monthly income less than 75 rubles.

Table 3 GDP per capita, 2000–22, current US dollars

	2000	2014	2016	2019	2020	2021	2022
Kazakhstan	1,229	12,807	7,715	9,813	9,122	10,374	11,492
Kyrgyz Republic	280	1,280	1,121	1,452	1,257	1,366	1,655
Tajikistan	138	1,104	807	889	852	917	1,054
Turkmenistan	643	7,962	6,398	7,180	7,297	7,885	8,793
Uzbekistan	558	2,492	2,568	1,795	1,759	1,993	2,255

Source: World Development Indicators at https://databank.worldbank.org/source/world-development-indicators (accessed 24 June 2024).

for migrant labour in Russia; in all five countries, output per head was much higher in 2014 than in 2000, before dropping sharply in 2015–16 (Table 3). After the end of the resource boom, governments sought to diversify the national economies amid challenges of the COVID-19 pandemic and the Russia-Ukraine war.

Despite the improved material living standards and social policies, the Soviet era was not viewed dispassionately. In the Soviet division of labour, Central Asia supplied primary products (cotton, minerals, and oil and gas) to the more developed republics (primarily Russia) in what was often viewed from Central Asia as a metropole-colonies arrangement. Moreover, the nature of the infrastructure, with railways, roads, pipelines, and telecommunications all connecting Central

Asia to Russia, created a geographical dependence. Finally, despite the creation of *homo sovieticus* and pride in Soviet successes such as victory in 1945 and Yuri Gagarin's first flight in space in 1961, there was still room for older loyalties that were reflected in anti-Russian demonstrations in Tashkent and Almaty.[32] Accompanying the economic progress since independence has been a redirection of economic relations away from dependence on Russia, which will be analysed in the next section.

3.1 Independence and the Transition from Central Planning

After independence, the central planning system broke down and in all former Soviet republics the 1990s were a decade of economic hardship. The initial collapse of the ruble zone and of public finance led to hyperinflation in the early 1990s. The breakdown of supply chains, as transport links between former republics were disrupted, exacerbated the recession associated with the transition to market-based economies. Uzbekistan had the shallowest recession, but domestic production only regained its 1989 level in 1999. In Kazakhstan, the Kyrgyz Republic and Turkmenistan, output in 1999 was about two-thirds of 1989 levels. Tajikistan had a more catastrophic decline as civil war lasted until 1997 and the central government only established control over the national territory in 2001.[33]

The variety of market-based economies established in Central Asia was substantial. Kyrgyzstan made the most fundamental reforms and established the least regulated market economy in the former Soviet Union; in 1998, it became the first former Soviet republic to join the WTO.[34] At the other extreme, Turkmenistan made few economic reforms, minimizing change other than transferring revenues from cotton and natural gas exports to the president's personal bank accounts. In the two largest economies, Kazakhstan was initially considered a reformist country but in the second half of the 1990s the president increasingly ruled by decree and the privatization process heightened wealth inequality, while Uzbekistan emphasized gradual reform that eased ongoing provision of public services but became associated with an increasingly heavy-handed government regulation. In Tajikistan the civil war was associated with

---

[32] After independence, Gagarin's spaceship was still on display in Kazakhstan's national museum.

[33] The GDP estimates of multilateral agencies like the International Monetary Fund, World Bank and European Bank for Reconstruction and Development are similar and as good as we have but must be treated with caution because the composition of output and of consumption changed greatly during the 1990s. Moreover, data collection was not a priority during the establishment of the new nations. Even for the twenty-first century some government data are unreliable, especially from Turkmenistan.

[34] The country's official name was changed from the Republic of Kyrgyzstan to the Kyrgyz Republic on 5 May 1993. Both names are in common use, and they are used interchangeably in this Element.

the collapse of government control, creating a market economy without supporting institutions such as legal support of property rights.

Uzbekistan benefited from its inherited administrative capacity as the metropolitan centre of Soviet Central Asia and coordinator of the cotton economy. Cotton was easily transportable and could be sold on the world market, where prices boomed up to 1996. Gold was also readily exportable, while other minerals were tied to the inherited rail network. Factories like the Kyrgyz sugar refinery closed once the cost of transporting Cuban cane sugar was included. Oil and gas exports used the Soviet pipelines, which left Turkmenistan dependent on customers who did not pay for their gas. At the oil prices of the 1990s, it made little economic sense to invest in large pipeline projects, although oil unlike natural gas could be shipped by rail and sea, for example, to Baku and then by pipeline to Georgian Black Sea ports.

International trade flows gradually shifted towards new markets and suppliers. In 1997, for the first time more than half of the Central Asian countries' international trade was with partners outside the former Soviet Union. Most of the new trade in the 1990s was with Europe, but after 2000 the share of China would increase rapidly.

3.2 The Resource Boom, 1999–2014

During the 1990s oil prices stagnated below $20 a barrel (Table 4 and Figure 1). After 1999, world prices of oil and of other resource exports such as gold, copper, and aluminium (but not cotton) soared, with slight differences in timing. Oil prices slumped in 2009 but rose again in 2010 and reached new highs in 2011. Another correction started in 2014 and prices fell below $60 in 2015 and 2016, accompanied by dramatic fall in value of the currencies of Russia and Kazakhstan. At this point, it was recognized that the resource boom was over and new economic development strategies were required.

Table 4 Oil prices; Brent dated prices in USD per barrel, 1991–2021

Year	Price	Year	Price	Year	Price	Year	Price
1992	*19.32*	2000	*28.50*	2008	*97.26*	2016	*43.37*
1993	*16.97*	2001	*24.44*	2009	*61.67*	2017	*54.19*
1994	*15.82*	2002	*25.02*	2010	*79.50*	2018	*71.31*
1995	*17.02*	2003	*28.83*	2011	*111.26*	2019	*64.21*
1996	*20.67*	2004	*38.27*	2012	*111.67*	2020	*41.84*
1997	*19.09*	2005	*54.52*	2013	*108.66*	2021	*70.91*
1998	*12.72*	2006	*65.14*	2014	*98.95*	2022	*101.32*
1999	*17.97*	2007	*72.39*	2015	*52.39*		

Source: BP *Statistical Review of World Energy 2023*, page 24.

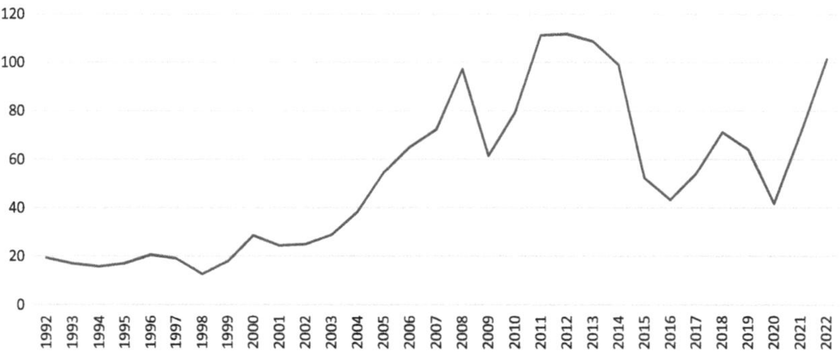

Figure 1 Oil prices; Brent dated prices in USD per barrel, 1991–2019

Pipelines were the dominant means of transport for oil and gas in the 1990s and 2000s. Kazakhstan's oil was transported north to refineries in Russia by the Russian company Transneft. The pricing by Transneft was unacceptable to the partners in the Tengiz oilfield, who invested in an alternative pipeline to the Black Sea – still through Russian territory – as well as shipping oil across the Caspian Sea to Baku and then by pipeline to Georgia's Black Sea port terminals. As the price of oil increased after 1999, proposals for alternative pipelines became feasible. In 2006, a pipeline from Baku to Ceyhan on Turkey's Mediterranean coast was completed and could be accessed by boat from Tengiz to Baku. In 2009, an overland pipeline from western Kazakhstan to China further increased the choice of transport routes. By the peak of the oil boom, Kazakh oil producers had a choice of export routes that left them independent of any single operator or government.

Turkmenistan's options for natural gas exports were more limited. In the 1990s, all the gas went through Russia to eventual destinations in Ukraine and Azerbaijan, with associated problems of payment by barter or simply non-payment. In the 2000s the situation improved slightly, but prices increased at a far slower speed than the prices received by Russia for gas exports to the EU (Global Witness, 2006). In 2006, Turkmenistan signed an agreement with China to build a gas pipeline which was completed in 2009. Since then, over 90 per cent of Turkmen exports have gone to China.

The resource boom had less dramatic impact on the other three countries' GDP (Table 3), but it was still a period of substantially rising incomes after the hardships of the 1990s. Uzbekistan was more or less self-sufficient in natural gas and benefited from high world prices for gold, copper, and other minerals. Tajikistan and the Kyrgyz Republic as energy importers suffered from higher oil and gas prices, but they benefited from higher prices for aluminium and gold. A major impact of the oil boom on the three countries was the increased demand for labour in Russia which led to around two million Uzbeks and a million Tajiks and a million Kyrgyz citizens working there; by 2013 Tajikistan had the world's highest ratio of remittances to GDP and the Kyrgyz Republic had the third highest.[35]

The fall of the oil prices began gradually in 2014, accelerated in 2015 and then stabilized in 2016; in Figure 1, this is captured by the average price dropping below $100 in 2014 and below $50 in 2016. Impacts on GDP in US dollars (and on remittances) were accentuated by large currency devaluations in Russia and later in Kazakhstan. The delayed impact in Uzbekistan in Table 3 was largely due to maintaining a stable exchange rate (supported by exchange controls and leading to a large premium on black market dollars). After the death of President Karimov in September 2016, Uzbekistan went through a period of reform that included major change in the exchange rate policy that eliminated the black market.

3.3 New Economic Directions and Regional Cooperation

During the boom years, there was a redirection of Central Asian trade as new customers or suppliers outside the CIS were identified. Between 2000 and 2010, Central Asian exports to the EU increased from $3.7 billion to $31.9 billion, or from 24% to 38% of total exports, while Russia's share slipped from 23% to 14% (Table 5). This was largely driven by the dominant role of EU firms in the oil and gas sector; the Italian firm Eni (AGIP) was the lead operator of Kazakhstan's offshore Kashagan oilfield, and French, British, and Dutch energy companies were also active in Kazakhstan.[36] Russia maintained its lead as a supplier of Central Asian imports, but China was catching up fast. Initially the China trade was mostly unrecorded imports by small-scale traders through entrepôts in the Kyrgyz Republic, but trade gradually became more formal.[37]

In the decade 2000–10, China established itself as a major economic partner. Transport links were improved almost from scratch, as new railways and roads connected Kazakhstan and the Kyrgyz Republic to China. Following the 1960 Sino-Soviet split the border between the USSR and western China was closed for almost thirty years. The first railway connection was completed in 1990 between

---

[35] World Bank: *Migration and Remittances Factbook 2016*, World Bank: Washington, DC.

[36] The dates in Table 5 do not correspond to the full period of the resource boom, but Mogilevskii's study is by far the most careful analysis of the often-opaque trade data of the period.

[37] The main entrepôts were two large bazaars outside the cities of Bishkek and Osh (Kaminski and Mitra, 2012). With an estimated 55,000 workers, including sellers and porters and those providing food, lodging, transport, and other services, the Dordoi market outside Bishkek may have been the world's largest shopping mall, measured by employment, in the early 2010s.

Table 5 Ten largest Central Asian export and import markets, 2000 and 2010 (in billion US dollars; numbers in parentheses are percentage shares)

Central Asian exports			Central Asian imports		
Destination	**2000**	**2010**	**Origin**	**2000**	**2010**
EU	3.7 (23.8)	31.9 (37.7)	Russia	3.1 (27.2)	17.2 (27.3)
Russia	3.6 (23.3)	13.8 (16.4)	EU	2.2 (19.0)	11.1 (17.5)
China	0.7 (4.8)	12.4 (14.6)	China	0.3 (2.4)	6.8 (10.7)
Iran	0.5 (3.3)	4.0 (4.8)	United States	0.6 (5.1)	4.1 (6.6)
Turkey	0.4 (2.5)	2.7 (3.1)	Turkey	0.5 (4.6)	2.5 (4.0)
Switzerland	0.6 (4.1)	1.7 (2.0)	S. Korea	0.4 (3.8)	2.2 (3.5)
United States	0.2 (1.5)	1.1 (1.3)	Pakistan	0.2 (1.3)	1.9 (3.1)
Japan	0.1 (0.5)	0.6 (0.7)	Iran	0.2 (2.0)	1.8 (2.8)
S. Korea	0.1 (0.9)	0.4 (0.4)	Japan	0.3 (3.0)	0.9 (1.4)
India	0.1 (0.4)	0.3 (0.3)	India	0.1 (0.9)	0.8 (1.3)

Source: Mogilevskii (2012, 30–31), based on data from COMTRADE and national statistical offices.

Notes: Totals include Afghanistan as well as the five Central Asian countries.

China and Kazakhstan and a second Kazakhstan-China rail link opened in 2013. Roads were closed until the Gorbachev era when they began to reopen gradually; after the turn of the century, road links were dramatically improved and Chinese-funded highways were built from the border to Bishkek and to Uzbekistan. Air connections between Urumqi and Almaty opened in the early 1990s.

Exports to China increased, especially in the case of Turkmenistan whose exports went overwhelmingly to China after completion of the gas pipeline in 2009. For Central Asia as a whole, the role of China was primarily as supplier of imports. As Central Asian incomes rose, demand for a large variety of consumer goods increased. These were exactly the kind of goods that the centrally planned economy had been poor at identifying and this was to some extent still true of the Russian and Central Asian economies, while China's rapid growth had been largely based on exports of such goods.

The end of the resource boom was followed by recognition of the need for a new economic strategy with less reliance on export of primary products. With small domestic markets, there was little scope for strategies focussing on domestic markets. Finding competitive new exports would, however, require reforms to facilitate international trade and reduce the costs of doing business. Such changes are easy to announce but often difficult to implement against opposition from vested interests who benefit from the existing policies. The role of the government in providing an economic environment conducive to entrepreneurs identifying export niches did not come easily to Central Asian leaders who had grown up in the centrally planned economy where officials determined the output mix.[38]

The new strategy required low costs in money and time of conducting international trade. This had not been a priority when export costs for primary products were specific to oil or gas or cotton. Yet in reports like the frequently referenced World Bank *Doing Business* indicators, the Central Asian countries ranked among the worst in the world for ease of trading across borders.[39] The more firmly based Corridor Performance Monitoring and Measurement (CPMM) data produced by the Central Asian Regional Economic Cooperation (CAREC) Secretariat highlighted the painfully slow travel times for trucks and trains in Central Asia when border crossing was involved.[40] Tackling this issue not only required domestic reforms (e.g. to simplify customs procedures) but also required regional cooperation to facilitate transport along important corridors passing through several countries.

The challenges were substantial. One positive feature was a generational shift in Central Asian leadership beginning in 2016 (Table 6). The new leadership was less Soviet-influenced, more comfortable with market-based economies, and more experienced in the world beyond Russia (Pomfret, 2021). The first-generation presidents were men who had spent their lives in the centrally planned Soviet Union and had risen to power through Soviet institutions. After becoming national presidents, they focused on nation-building with little interest in foreign relations beyond photo opportunities; they were often scarcely on speaking terms with other Central Asian presidents. While the first presidents were bilingual in Russian and their republic's national language, the current leaders are more likely

---

[38] Some examples from East Asia illustrate the point. When Hong Kong began its export-led growth in the 1950s and 1960s leading exports included artificial flowers and false eyelashes; the entrepreneur who identified these niches, Li Ka-shing (later the richest man in Hong Kong) also knew when to move on as fashions changed. In China's initial switch to export-led growth in the 1980s, successful township and village enterprises identified export niches like Christmas tree lights and dog leashes. None of these items would have been identified by central planners. The Hong Kong and Chinese exporters responded to policies that allowed them to import inputs and to export with minimal red tape.

[39] In the 2015 *Doing Business* report, which covered 189 countries' ease of international trade in June 2014, the Kyrgyz Republic ranked 183rd, Kazakhstan 185th, Tajikistan 188th, and Uzbekistan 189th; Turkmenistan was not included but would have been worse than Uzbekistan. www.doing business.org/content/dam/doingBusiness/media/Annual-Reports/English/DB15-Full-Report.pdf .

[40] Corruption is an issue in all five countries but is difficult to document and takes varied forms. Cooley and Heathershaw (2019) document the links between the corrupt elites and facilitators who help launder their money through international financial centres. The widespread demonstrations in Kazakhstan in January 2022 were, in large part, responses to the wealth accumulated by President Nazarbayev's family and associates. In the Transparency International Corruption Perceptions Index, the Central Asian countries always rank in the bottom half of the surveyed countries with Kazakhstan appearing as the least corrupt and Turkmenistan the most corrupt of the five countries (Khitakhunov, 2021), perhaps reflecting a contrast between the grand larceny in resource-rich Kazakhstan and Turkmenistan and the more ubiquitous corruption elsewhere in Central Asia.

Table 6 Central Asian leaders by date of birth, 1991 and 2023

	December 1991		December 2023	
	Name	**Date of birth**	**Name**	**Date of birth**
Kazakhstan	Nazarbayev	1940	Tokayev	1953
Kyrgyz Republic	Akayev	1944	Japarov	1968
Tajikistan	Nabiyev	1930	Rahmon	1953
Turkmenistan	Niyazov	1940	Berdimuhamedov	1957
Uzbekistan	Karimov	1938	Mirziyoyev	1957

Source: updated from Pomfret (2021).

Notes: Tajik President Rahmon is expected to abdicate in favour of his son, Rustam Emomali, born in 1987. The other older president, Tokayev, had been exposed to non-Soviet economies as a Soviet diplomat at embassies in Singapore and Beijing before 1992.

to speak English, and in Tokayev's case Chinese, as well as Russian.[41] This mirrors similar changes in the wider population and in human capital. In sum, current leadership is more comfortable with participation in the global economy than the first presidents, and their populations will be more comfortable with external relations beyond Russia.[42]

The internal orientation of the first-generation leaders did, however, provide an important precondition for the more positive approach to regional cooperation after 2017. The respect for inherited national borders in Central Asia contrasted with other parts of the former Soviet Union where externally supported secession (Abkhazia and South Ossetia, Crimea, Nagorno Karabagh, and Transdniestria) or interstate war (Armenia versus Azerbaijan) soured international relations. Respect for territorial integrity was not inevitable; Tajikistan still considers the loss of Bukhara and Samarkand after the dissolution of the Emirate of Bukhara in the 1920s a national disaster, and Uzbekistan could have supported Uzbek minorities in all their neighbours (Table 1). Groups that

---

[41] It may be argued that corrupt Central Asian presidents found an autocrat like President Putin a more congenial counterpart than leaders who worry about democracy and human rights. Such attitudes played a role in Uzbekistan's switch from GUAM to the CSTO in 2005–8, but the argument does not seem generally true for the current generation of Central Asian presidents. Moreover, Russia is not the only semi-democratic or autocratic partner to be found in fora like the SCO.

[42] As a result of the Bolashak Program established in 1993 to finance undergraduate or postgraduate education abroad for competitively selected students, Kazakhstan now has about 16,000 well-educated young citizens with international views and experience. Leading domestic universities in Kazakhstan, Kyrgyzstan, and Uzbekistan have improved substantially in the twenty-first century.

failed to obtain full republic status in the Soviet Union have retained some degree of autonomy and, although not always content, neither the Republic of Karakalpakstan nor Gorno-Badakhshan Autonomous Province fought to secede as Nagorno Karabagh did (as the Republic of Artsakh between 1994 and 2023). The Ferghana Valley is an ethnic patchwork where neighbouring villages of differing ethnicity may come to blows, but national leaders prevented violent outbreaks from turning into international wars.[43]

Disputes did arise, especially over water. Uzbekistan strongly opposed Tajikistan's massive Rogun Dam project as a threat to the availability of water to irrigate downstream cottonfields. An indicator of the new environment after Uzbek President Islam Karimov's death in September 2016 was the acceptance by his successor, Shafkat Mirziyoyev, of the dam project and an offer to negotiate with Tajikistan over the joint consequences, rather than to threaten dire reprisals if President Emomali Rahmon continued with his signature policy. When Uzbekistan's Sardoba Dam burst in May 2020, flooding a large area of Uzbekistan and southern Kazakhstan and requiring the evacuation of over 30,000 people in Kazakhstan, President Mirziyoyev and Kazakhstan President Kassym-Jomart Tokayev, who had succeeded President Nazarbayev six months earlier, were in contact the day after the disaster, working on joint disaster management without recriminations.[44]

Since 2017, improved relations between the five Central Asian leaders have been institutionalized in Central Asian Summits in Almaty, Kazakhstan (2018), Tashkent, Uzbekistan (2019), Avaza, Turkmenistan (2021), Cholpon-Ata, Kyrgyz Republic (2022), and Dushanbe, Tajikistan (2023). The five leaders have also collaborated in concerted actions in other fora. The 5+1 format was initiated at the December 2019 meeting in Delhi between the five Central Asian presidents and Prime Minister Narendra Modi. After the break in face-to-face meetings in 2020–1 due to COVID-19, the 5+1 format was revived in meetings with the European Union; the November 2022 EU-Central Asia Connectivity Conference in Samarkand was attended by the EU High Representative for Foreign Affairs and the foreign ministers of the five Central Asian countries, and the June 2023 Cholpon-Ata high-level meeting with President of the European Council Charles Michel included a commitment to an EU-Central Asian summit in Uzbekistan in 2024. A January 2022 virtual summit with

---

[43] The Kyrgyz-Tajik border has seen several small but violent episodes since 2021, most notably in September 2022 when over thirty people died. However, the two countries' presidents acted quickly to defuse tensions.

[44] Initial tensions on Kazakh social media were assuaged by Uzbekistan's immediate response in sending fire engines, excavators, tractors, and other equipment to the flooded area of Kazakhstan. Five days after the disaster, Uzbek Prime Minister Abdulla Aripov travelled to Kazakhstan to monitor assistance in the affected area where he met Kazakh Prime Minister Askar Mamin.

China's President Xi Jinping was followed by an in-person C+C5 summit in Xian in May 2023. In September 2023, a C5+1 Presidential summit with US President Joseph Biden took place in New York.[45] The 2023 C5+1 meetings with the two Superpower leaders would have been unimaginable a few years earlier. The C5 format asserted a shared self-confidence and self-image whether through history, geography, or culture. And this shared vision did not include Russia.

4 Redirected Economic Relations and Multi-vector Foreign Policies

As the Soviet Union was dissolved in December 1991, Kazakhstan's President Nazarbayev played an active role in trying to retain Soviet-era connections. Based on the Belovezh Accords signed on 8 December 1991 between Russia, Belarus, and Ukraine, the Alma-Ata Protocol on 21 December brought eight other former Soviet republics into the CIS. When Georgia joined in 1993, the CIS included all former Soviet republics except the three Baltic countries. Turkmenistan never ratified the CIS agreement; by 1995 Turkmenistan's central foreign policy tenet was neutrality, which was embodied in a motion at the United Nations, although in 2005 Turkmenistan became an associate member of the CIS. The other Central Asian countries remain full CIS members and all have signed the CIS Free Trade Agreement.

The Collective Security Treaty was signed in May 1992 in Tashkent by Armenia, Kazakhstan, Kyrgyzstan, Russia, Tajikistan and Uzbekistan, and Azerbaijan, Georgia and Belarus joined subsequently. In April 1999, the Protocol on prolongation of the Collective Security Treaty was signed by six of the countries (Azerbaijan, Georgia, and Uzbekistan did not sign) and the Collective Security Treaty Organization (CSTO) was transformed into a full-fledged international organization in May 2002. Uzbekistan joined the CSTO in 2005 and left in 2008. Although the Central Asian countries remain connected to the CIS and Kazakhstan, Kyrgyzstan, and Tajikistan are in the CSTO, the influence of these Russian-led organizations has diminished since the 1990s.[46]

---

[45] The C5+1 Leaders' Joint Statement *The New York Declaration: C5+1 Resilience through Security, Economic, and Energy Partnership* is posted at www.whitehouse.gov/briefing-room/statements-releases/2023/09/21/c51-leaders-joint-statement/.

[46] An apparent exception to this generalization was the request from Kazakhstan's government for CSTO assistance in dealing with unrest that broke out in early January 2022. The CSTO, for the first time answered a call for aid and deployed some 2,500 troops to guard key facilities but only in a few cities, and for less than two weeks. The episode appears to have been a panic reaction by President Tokayev who feared a threat to his position, but who soon realized that the demonstrations were against his predecessor and people who had become rich under President Nazarbayev. A striking sign of the CSTO's weakness was Russia's failure to come to the aid of CSTO-signatory

Many trade agreements were signed among the Central Asian countries in the 1990s and 2000s, but with little impact.[47] The general pattern was of continued participation by Kazakhstan, the Kyrgyz Republic, and Tajikistan in Russian-led initiatives, such as the Eurasian Economic Community, with Uzbekistan vacillating and Turkmenistan remaining neutral. The practical significance of the economic agreements changed with the establishment of a customs union between Russia, Belarus, and Kazakhstan after 2010 and its deepening into the EAEU in 2015, when Armenia and the Kyrgyz Republic also joined.

Other agreements had little economic content. The Shanghai Cooperation Organization, however, included both Russia and China and for the Central Asian members China's presence in the SCO was a useful counterweight to Russian political influence. The Central Asian countries refused to acknowledge in 2008 the independence of South Ossetia and Abkhazia and in 2014 the absorption of Crimea into Russia, in both cases following China's abstention in UN votes.

The general pattern has been an evolution from all Central Asian countries being initially involved in the Russian-led CIS, but Turkmenistan and then Uzbekistan and finally Tajikistan becoming less willing to participate in Russian-led organizations (e.g. in the CSTO or EAEU). Even Kazakhstan and the Kyrgyz Republic appear to have become less enthusiastic about the EAEU. These political developments reflect changes in economic relations, in which Russia has become less dominant over the three decades since independence, and since 2019 foreign policy has been increasingly conducted in 5+1 format, by which the five Central Asian countries deal jointly with other countries.

4.1 Multi-vector Diplomacy

As a counterpart to the diversification of economic partners, the leaders of Kazakhstan, Uzbekistan, and the Kyrgyz Republic adopted multi-vector diplomacy, that is, maintaining links with a range of external partners. Although the United States remained a minor trade partner, US firms were strategic investors, especially in Kazakh oil and agricultural equipment. After 9/11, Central Asia supplied important services in support of the US military in Afghanistan through the northern distribution network (Yuldasheva, 2013) and through the

---

Armenia during its 2020 war with Azerbaijan or over the disarmament of the separatist Armenian militias in Nagorno Karabakh in September 2023.

[47] The new independent countries were not concerned about market access, because their exports were concentrated in a handful of commodities (cotton, oil and gas, gold, and other minerals) which could be sold duty-free on world markets, and they wanted to maintain control over regulating imports. While they all joined international organizations that did not require commitments, only Kyrgyzstan joined the WTO in the 1990s.

rent of airport facilities in Uzbekistan until 2005 and in the Kyrgyz Republic until 2014. Relations with China and the EU were cultivated as counterweights to Russian influence.

The new independent states of Central Asia continued to look to Russia as the senior economic partner, although in the 1990s symbolic links like the common currency, the Cyrillic script, and use of Russian as the *lingua franca* all withered. The common currency was abandoned in 1993. The Cyrillic script was replaced by variations of the Latin script by Turkmenistan on independence and by Uzbekistan in September 1993.[48] Russian is still widely understood and used as a common language in meetings among Central Asians, but younger generations are more likely to acquire English as their second language. At the same time, Russia's position as a senior partner was not under threat in the 1990s. The United States opened embassies in all five countries but provided little economic assistance. The EU provided technical assistance through the Technical Assistance to the Commonwealth of Independent States (TACIS) program, but the funding was small, and the flagship Transport Connecting Central Asia and the Caucasus (TRACECA) program had little impact. Physical links with China had been virtually non-existent since the 1960s; the first rail connection from Kazakhstan to China was only completed in 1990 and road crossings gradually reopened in the 1990s. China was quietly building confidence in the context of border delimitation negotiations with Russia, Kazakhstan, Kyrgyzstan, and Tajikistan, the so-called Shanghai Five, named after the location of the negotiations.[49] In sum, the region benefited from its insignificance for outside powers during the first post-independence decade.

The 2000s saw a revival of the Russian economy and interest in Central Asia, but also renewed US interest in the region driven by the 2001 invasion of Afghanistan. Initially, Russia acquiesced in US forces having bases in Central Asia and more broadly supplying US troops through the northern distribution network. Thus, for the decade of the 2000s, the Central Asian countries were able to balance the influence of Russia and the United States; leaders like President Nazarbayev could make official visits and meet the presidents of both the United States and Russia. At

---

[48] Kazakhstan has announced that it too will shift to the Latin script. Similar proposals have been floated in Kyrgyzstan but are opposed by President Sadyr Japarov.

[49] My personal experience from conferences and workshops in the 1990s with CIS and PRC participants was that former Soviet officials looked down on China as a poor country with nothing to offer them and PRC delegates looked down on the former Soviet officials as failed managers of a stagnant economic system. Three decades of separation after the Sino-Soviet split also bred racist clichés based on stereotypes rather than experience. The Shanghai Five meetings were an important step in confidence-building in the 1990s, when trade flows between China and Central Asia were still small (Table 5).

the same time, the EU was the major trade partner during the resource boom, and China's importance as an economic partner was rising rapidly.

Russia's relations with Georgia in 2008 and Ukraine in 2014 soured as Russia supported separatism in Abkhazia and South Ossetia and in Donetsk and Luhansk, and annexed Crimea after a dubious referendum. Russian policy within the former Soviet Union became more selective in 2010 as it moved to strengthen relations with Belarus and Kazakhstan by creating a customs union. In 2015, the customs union was deepened and widened to become the EAEU with Armenia and the Kyrgyz Republic joining the three original members. Tajikistan was pressured by Russia to join but refused, despite offers of improved treatment of the million Tajik migrant workers in Russia.

Assessment of the EAEU has been mixed both from the Central Asian members and from outsiders.[50] The economic impact of EAEU membership on Kazakhstan and the Kyrgyz Republic was negative as the customs union's common external tariffs were largely based on Russia's tariffs, which meant that both the Central Asian countries had to raise their pre-accession tariffs.[51] However, beyond the common external tariff, EAEU members do not appear bound by a common policy.[52] On a political level, Kazakhstan and the Kyrgyz Republic appeared lukewarm towards the EAEU after the end of the resource boom.

The two Central Asian members of the EAEU did benefit from sanctions imposed on Russia after February 2022. A substantial amount of trade between EU countries and Russia was diverted through Kazakhstan and the Kyrgyz Republic (Chupilkin et al., 2023; Hugot and Mogilevskii, 2023). There were also brain and financial drains as Russians evaded financial sanctions by opening bank accounts in Central Asia or by emigrating, although such flows did not necessarily benefit EAEU members more than non-members such as Uzbekistan.[53]

---

[50] The customs union was initially promoted as a counterpart to the EU with potential to create free trade from Lisbon to Vladivostok. However, EU interest was negligible, especially as transformation from customs union to economic union followed Russia's 2014 annexation of Crimea (Arynov, 2023).

[51] This posed a serious legal problem for the Kyrgyz Republic which had bound its tariffs at lower levels when the country joined the World Trade Organization in 1998. Kazakhstan did not join the WTO until November 2015.

[52] The lack of EAEU solidarity is explicit in the WTO negotiations on digital trade, where Russia and Kazakhstan are among the 80+ countries signed up to the e-commerce Joint Statement while the Kyrgyz Republic and Armenia are not (Belarus is not a WTO member).

[53] Between January and September 2022, the number of Russian companies in Kazakhstan increased by around 4,000 (Monteiro-Benson, 2023). In the week following President Putin's partial mobilization order on 21 September 2022, around 98,000 Russians fled to Kazakhstan (Dasha Litvinova 'Over 194,000 Russians flee call-up to neighboring countries', Associated Press 27 September 2022 at https://apnews.com/article/russia-ukraine-putin-estonia-kazakhstan-d851fdd9e99bedbf4e01 b98efd18d14b). Following a backlash against immigrants, the Kazakh authorities imposed stay limits on EAEU visitors and required Kazakh language proficiency for residence permits, prompting many to move on to Tashkent where restrictions were less strict.

One sign of limited commitment to the EAEU has been the signing of agreements with the European Union. Such steps had triggered Russia's more belligerent attitude towards Ukraine, but that did not deter Kazakhstan from signing an Enhanced Partnership and Cooperation Agreement (EPCA) with the EU in 2016. The agreement aims to bring the EU partner's arrangements in line with EU regulations, although the EPCA does not affect Kazakhstan's tariffs, which are the EAEU common external tariff. In 2022 the EU and Uzbekistan signed an EPCA, and the Kyrgyz Republic is negotiating an EPCA with the EU. Such regulatory alignment facilitates trade and other economic relations with the EU, and the 'Brussels Effect' has been seen as a soft power instrument bringing countries closer to the EU (Bradford, 2020).

4.2 Relations with China and the EU

Central Asia's economic relations with China and the EU have been primarily driven by trade and foreign investment. Aggregate trade values are dominated by Kazakhstan's exports of oil to the EU which reflect the leading role of European energy majors in developing the Kashagan offshore oil field, the Karachaganak gas deposits, and other energy projects. China imports raw materials (notably coal and iron from Kazakhstan and gas from Turkmenistan) and has become Central Asia's leading source of manufactured imports.

Since 2011, Central Asia has become an increasingly important part of overland transport links between the EU and China. The main line between Chongqing and Duisburg transits Kazakhstan, Russia, Belarus, and Poland (Map 4). Success depended on coordination between national rail companies and customs services, and required some investment (e.g. at the change of gauge points), but the trains used existing track, and the process was primarily demand-driven. Major customers included car and electronics companies seeking to connect their European and Asian supply chains and willing to pay for the higher cost of rail versus sea in return for faster and more reliable delivery times.

Rail traffic along the Landbridge increased dramatically (Table 7), and transit fees became a major foreign income source for Kazakhstan. By 2016, the Duisburg–Chongqing service was daily; freight forwarders and others provided added services (part-container loads, refrigerated containers, and onward multi-modal connections) that attracted an increasing array of customers in both directions. By 2017, more than thirty Chinese cities were termini for rail freight trains to and from the EU and roughly the same number of cities were termini in Europe. China's interest in the Landbridge was highlighted by President Xi's proposal, announced in October 2013 in Astana, for substantial investment in a Silk Road Economic Belt, which would be formally launched as the Belt

Table 7 Volume of traffic on China-EU and EU-China container trains, 2011–21

Year	Number of twenty-foot equivalent containers (TEUs)	Number of trains to and from China
2011		17
2012		42
2013		80
2014		308
2015	46,000	815
2016	100,500	1,702
2017	175,800	3,673
2018	280,500	6,376
2019	333,000	8,225
2020	546,900	12,406
2021	692,500	15,000

Sources: Pomfret (2024) based on: Column 1 – UTLC website at www.utlc.com; Column 2 – Chinese official data cited in *The 2021 Silk Road numbers are there: what do they tell us?* Posted at https://www.railfreight.com/specials/2022/01/14/the-2021-silk-road-numbers-are-here-what-do-they-tell-us/ 14 January 2022.

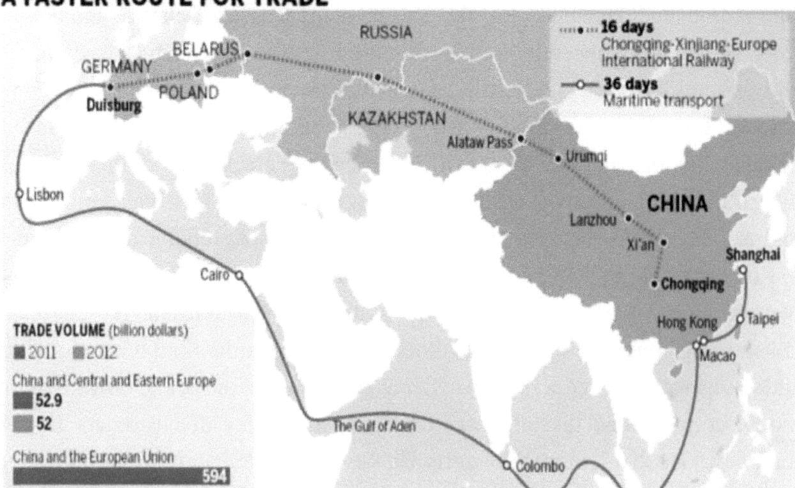

Map 4 The Chongqing–Duisburg Landbridge

Sources: Ministry of Commerce, General Administration of Customs, and YuXinCu Rail Logistics Company

component of the Belt and Road Initiative in May 2017 and become the centrepiece of China's international economic diplomacy.[54] The COVID pandemic in 2020–1 increased the attractiveness of the Eurasian Landbridge as maritime services were disrupted by quarantine and other problems.

Both the EU and China were supportive of a Eurasian connection. The principal EU assistance during the 1990s had been the TRACECA program; that initiative was premature, but the interest remained and revived after the EU transport network policy (TEN-T) reached the Black Sea. The main line north of the Caspian Sea had an obvious advantage over the TRACECA route which involved mode changes from rail to sea to cross the Caspian Sea and again to cross the Black Sea. At the same time, the northern route had the disadvantage of dependence on transit countries that might use their monopoly position to raise transit fees. Already exploring alternative routes, following the easing of UN sanctions on Iran in 2016, China initiated services through Kazakhstan and Turkmenistan to Tehran. However, the decrepit state of track between Iran and eastern Türkiye made this a poor option for traffic to the Middle East or Europe.

An alternative was the Middle Corridor from China to Baku and then either overland to Istanbul or crossing the Black Sea to Bulgaria or Romania (Map 5). The Middle Corridor was an improvement over the TRACECA route of the 1990s due to the upgrading of rail components and Caspian ports, including an improved east-west line across Kazakhstan cutting hundreds of kilometres from the route, the Baku–Tbilisi–Kars (BTK) line becoming operational in 2017 and providing a reliable connection to the Turkish rail network, and the Marmaray Tunnel under the Bosporus. However, the Middle Corridor attracted less than 5 per cent of Landbridge freight in 2021. The changes in mode, rail-sea-rail, remained an unattractive feature and a Black Sea crossing from Georgia to Romania or onward rail from Istanbul to Europe still had problems (e.g. transiting non-EU countries).

The EU also increased focus on the Middle Corridor, although it moves more slowly than China. In 2019–20 the EU announced the intention to bring its Trans-European Transport Network (TEN-T) in line with EU-China links.[55] Revisions of TEN-T regulations announced in April 2022 focused on standardizing infrastructure for longer and heavier trains along the TEN-T network, elevating punctuality of freight trains and enabling the crossing of internal EU borders within 15 minutes, and modernizing intermodal terminals. Application

---

[54] The continuing importance of the BRI and of Kazakhstan was highlighted by President Xi's choice of first foreign visit after the COVID lockdown. In September 2022, en route to the SCO summit in Samarkand, President Xi made a point of stopping over in Astana and giving a major speech.

[55] In 2019, the EU also announced a deepening of its partnership with Central Asia: www.eeas .europa.eu/sites/default/files/factsheet_centralasia_2019.pdf.

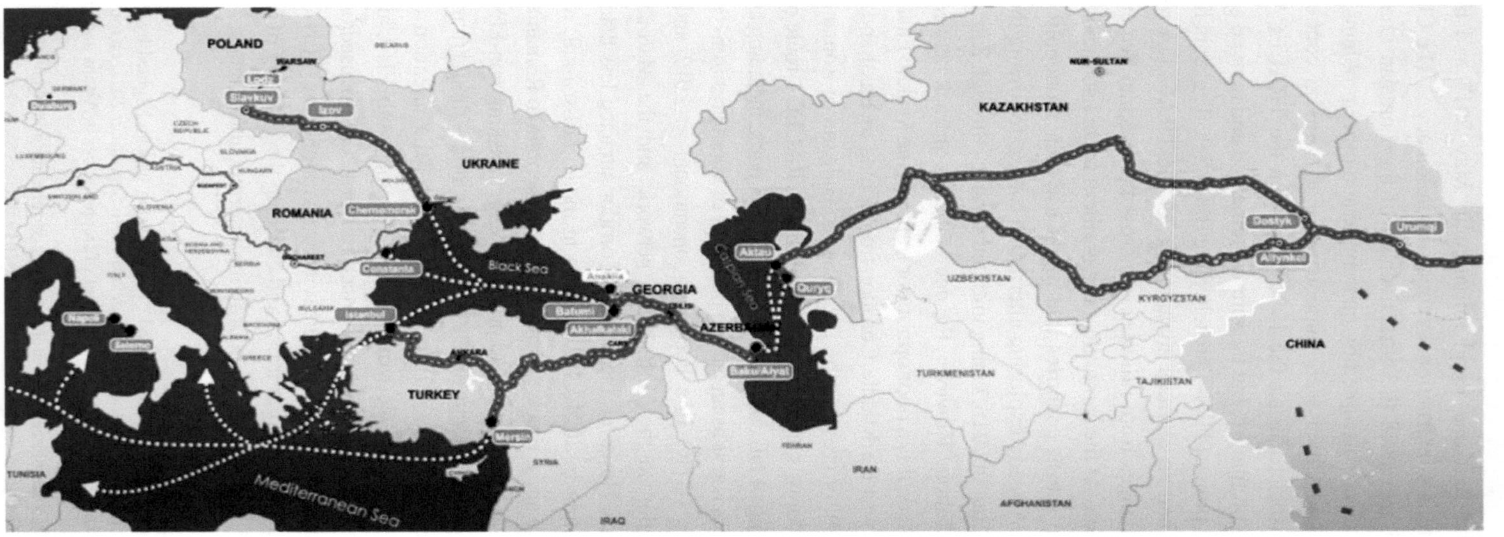

Map 5 Middle Corridor routes, March 2022

Source: reprinted with permission of the Middle Corridor Association (www.middlecorridor.com).

of the revised regulations aimed to ensure higher speeds and more reliable delivery times along rail freight corridors, which had been gradually extended to reach the Black Sea ports of Bulgaria and Romania.

4.3 Responses to Russian Expansion (Georgia 2008, Ukraine 2014 and 2022)

As the Central Asian countries recovered from the transitional recession of the 1990s and developed new markets, Russia's economic importance for the region diminished. The process varied across the five countries. For Kazakhstan, the crucial development was the construction of new pipelines that ended Russia's monopoly over oil export routes. At the same time, geography meant that Kazakhstan remained linked to Russia for imports, grain exports, and finance. In the open Kyrgyz economy, official and unofficial trade flourished as the Dordoi and Karasu bazaars became trading centres for local and Chinese sellers and customers from the Kyrgyz Republic and its three Central Asian neighbours. For Turkmenistan, with exports dominated by gas, dependence on Russia remained high until 2009, when it was replaced by dependence on China as an export market. Uzbekistan, with the most diversified economy in Central Asia, was best placed to maintain political distance from Russia. The only significant counter-trend between 2000 and 2014 was the increasing dependence of Tajikistan and the Kyrgyz Republic, and to a lesser extent Uzbekistan, on remittances from migrant workers in Russia.

When the first call for political support came from Russia after the 2008 war with Georgia, the five Central Asian governments were unanimous in refusing to acknowledge the independence of Abkhazia or South Ossetia. Of course, they had self-interest in not condoning infringement of a sovereign country's territorial integrity, but they had no special link to Georgia. The shared position with China, expressed at the SCO summit, gave some cover. Nevertheless, refusal to support Russia in 2008 contrasted with acquiescence to Russian involvement in secession during the frozen conflicts of the 1990s (Nagorno-Karabagh and Transdniestria). Lack of support for Russia was even clearer in 2014, when Russia annexed Crimea after a rapid referendum.[56]

In 2022, the five countries all declined to vote against the UN motion criticizing the Russian invasion of Ukraine; Turkmenistan and Uzbekistan did not vote, and the other three countries abstained. Addressing Uzbekistan's Senate on 17 March, Foreign Minister Abdulaziz Kamilov said that 'firstly, the military actions and

---

[56] For Kazakhstan, an added feature was that in 1992 Ukraine had signed a treaty guaranteeing its territorial integrity in return for decommissioning of nuclear weapons on its territory. Kazakhstan had signed a similar treaty and was unhappy to see how easily it could be broken.

violence must be stopped right away. The Republic of Uzbekistan recognises Ukraine's independence, sovereignty, and territorial integrity. We do not recognise the Luhansk and Donetsk republics'.[57] In June 2022, responding to a question at the Saint Petersburg Economic Forum while sitting next to President Putin, President Tokayev stated that Kazakhstan would not follow Russia in recognizing the independence of the Luhansk and Donetsk National Republics.[58] The Kyrgyz Republic and Tajikistan, with their large migrant workforce in Russia, were more cautious but unwilling to provide support.

4.4 The Russia-Ukraine War and the Landbridge

Landbridge trade began to be paused or rerouted in January 2022 as Ukraine-Russia tensions mounted and were more seriously hit when sanctions were imposed after the Russian invasion. The financial and export sanctions imposed by the United States and the EU on Russia on Friday 25 February meant that European companies could face issues with money transactions when doing business in Russia. A few days later, both the EU and United States added Russian Railways to their sanctions lists. Customers began abandoning the northern corridor, concerned about the legal implications of working with a sanctioned company and about potential problems such as insurance coverage being invalidated by 'Act of War' clauses.[59]

Alternatives to transiting Russia were sought immediately. In late February 2022, a train went from China to Istanbul and then the containers went by sea to Trieste. The Istanbul-Trieste segment avoided delays in southeast Europe at non-EU borders and due to rail works in Slovenia. This example highlights that, after traversing the Caspian Sea, the Middle Corridor typically involves a further sea crossing (Map 5). Destinations in the EU can be reached either by crossing the Black Sea from Georgia to enter the EU through Romania or Bulgaria or by crossing the Adriatic Sea from Istanbul or the Mediterranean Sea from Mersin to avoid passing through

---

[57] Quoted in the article *Ukraine war: Is Central Asia loosening ties with Russia?* posted on 25 March 2022 at www.aljazeera.com/news/2022/3/25/ukraine-war-is-central-asia-loosening-ties-with-russia (Accessed 15 September 2023).

[58] Kazakhstan, with a substantial Russian-speaking population near its long border with Russia, was considered more likely to avoid such direct confrontation and Tokayev was politically indebted to Putin for responding to his request for assistance from the Russian-led Collective Security Organization in addressing widespread protests in Kazakhstan five months earlier.

[59] The actual situation is difficult to assess. Arvis et al. (2022, 42) report that rail connections continued to function and, to avoid international payments to Russian Railways, freight charges could be paid in China. The ULTC website continued to report substantial traffic: 614,100 TEUs over the first eleven months of 2022. However, informed commentators saw a larger decline in EU-China-EU traffic, with variation in EU countries' sanctions compliance; Zhao (2023) found substantial decline in use of the Landbridge in 2022 by Belgium and the Netherlands while eastbound freight from Germany only fell by a fifth.

non-EU members in southeast Europe. Mersin can also be a gateway to the Middle East and North Africa; the Middle Corridor route to Mersin was used to send Chinese humanitarian aid (tents, etc.) to victims of the February 2023 earthquake in the Turkey-Syria border area.

The TITR (Trans-Caspian International Transport Route Association) reported 33,700 TEUs shipped along the Middle Corridor in 2022, a 34 per cent increase over 2021 but this was less than 10 per cent of reported traffic along the main Landbridge lines in 2022.[60] Scaling up the Middle Corridor faced capacity constraints associated with the Caspian Sea crossing as well as congestion at Constanta port in Romania and on parts of the Turkish rail network. The two boats operating between Azerbaijan and Kazakhstan at the start of 2022 had a combined capacity of 250 containers, that is, freight from five or six trains. A third ship with capacity of 350 containers was operating in April 2022. With a transit time of 3–4 days per round-trip, the three vessels could provide five departures per week and a maximum capacity of 1,450 containers, which is equivalent to 30–40 trains. With the addition of three new ships in September, this capacity doubled to 60–80 trains per week – a substantial increase, but still less than a quarter of the northern corridor traffic in 2021 (Table 7). Constanta faced congestion because freight previously intended to pass through Odesa to Ukraine or to Moldova shifted to Constanta.

For Middle Corridor countries, interest is driven by the potential transit fees. On 31 March 2022, Georgia, Azerbaijan, Türkiye, and Kazakhstan agreed to create a joint venture that would provide high-quality intermodal transport and logistics services, harmonize cross-border rates, and introduce a unified IT platform to fully automate cargo transport services from China to Türkiye, and the Black Sea ports. The statement emphasized the importance of cooperation between the countries along the route and of investment in infrastructure development to integrate the Trans-Caspian transport corridor into the international transport system. A priority is to accelerate works to increase the capacity of the Baku–Tbilisi–Kars (BTK) rail line.

The EU commitment to Central Asia and infrastructure investment in the region was restated in October 2022 when President of the European Council Charles Michel visited Kazakhstan and Uzbekistan.[61] The EU-Central Asia

---

[60] Both numbers are subject to question; the UTLC figures for 2022 have been frequently adjusted, and the Middle Corridor figures are only for traffic through Kazakhstan, as in Figure 5, ignoring the smaller but non-negligible traffic through Turkmenistan, as in Figure 6, but the relative magnitudes are unlikely to be far out (Pomfret, 2024).

[61] The press statement with Uzbekistan President Shavkat Mirziyoyev emphasized: 'Creation of sustainable transport corridors has been specified as key factor for increasing mutual trade, including explore options for further development of the Trans-Caspian Multimodal Route... The Presidents discussed the importance of expanding port capacities, increasing ferry and rail fleets, harmonizing customs procedures, introducing digital solutions for cargo handling and border crossing'.

Connectivity Conference in Samarkand in November 2022 was attended by the EU High Representative for Foreign Affairs, Josep Borrell, and the foreign ministers of the five Central Asian countries. Earlier in 2022, the EU funded a study by the European Bank for Reconstruction and Development of *Sustainable transport connections between Europe and Central Asia*; the Final Report, released on 16 June 2023, estimated priority infrastructure investment needs in the order of €18.5 billion.

4.5 Implications of Alternative Eurasian Rail Routes

The northern Landbridge was a substantial source of service exports for Kazakhstan. The value was reported by the Asian Development Bank to have been $1 billion in 2015 and, although subsequent values were considered commercially sensitive, the transit fees reached $2–4 billion by the end of the decade. However, all the traffic was in transit and the route did not provide an outlet for Central Asian goods exports. The situation along the Middle Corridor is already different.

Kazakhstan has used the TransCaspian route for grain, oil, minerals, and uranium for many years, and the route's popularity was increased by the Russia-Ukraine war. Kazakhstan sent new export products through the Middle Corridor, for example, twenty containers of lentils to Türkiye in January 2023. In September 2022, a train from Uzbekistan used the Middle Corridor to carry twenty-four 40-foot containers mainly filled with fertilizers via Turkmenistan, Azerbaijan, and Georgia across the Black Sea to Constanta (Romania). In December 2022, a train with forty-six containers of copper concentrate left Tashkent for Burgas (Bulgaria), a train of fertilizers went from Uzbekistan via Turkmenistan-Azerbaijan-Georgia to Lithuania, and a train from Izmir (Türkiye) brought household appliances to Tashkent.[62] Clothing importers in Tajikistan shipped jeans from Türkiye along the Middle Corridor.

Agreement on the route and financing of a rail link between Kashgar (Kashi), the furthest west point in China's rail network, and Uzbekistan via the Kyrgyz Republic was announced at the Samarkand summit of the Shanghai Cooperation Organization in September 2022. The project had been long proposed by Uzbekistan and supported by the Kyrgyz Republic, subject to others financing it. China had been lukewarm until 2022. The line will provide an alternative east-west route to the Caspian, avoiding both Russia and Kazakhstan and reducing journey times to southern Europe and to the Middle East and North Africa. Although not indicated in Map 6, several rail lines to the east link Kashgar to China's large cities and Kashgar is the

---

[62] Pomfret (2024) provides more details on the evidence reported in this and the next paragraph.

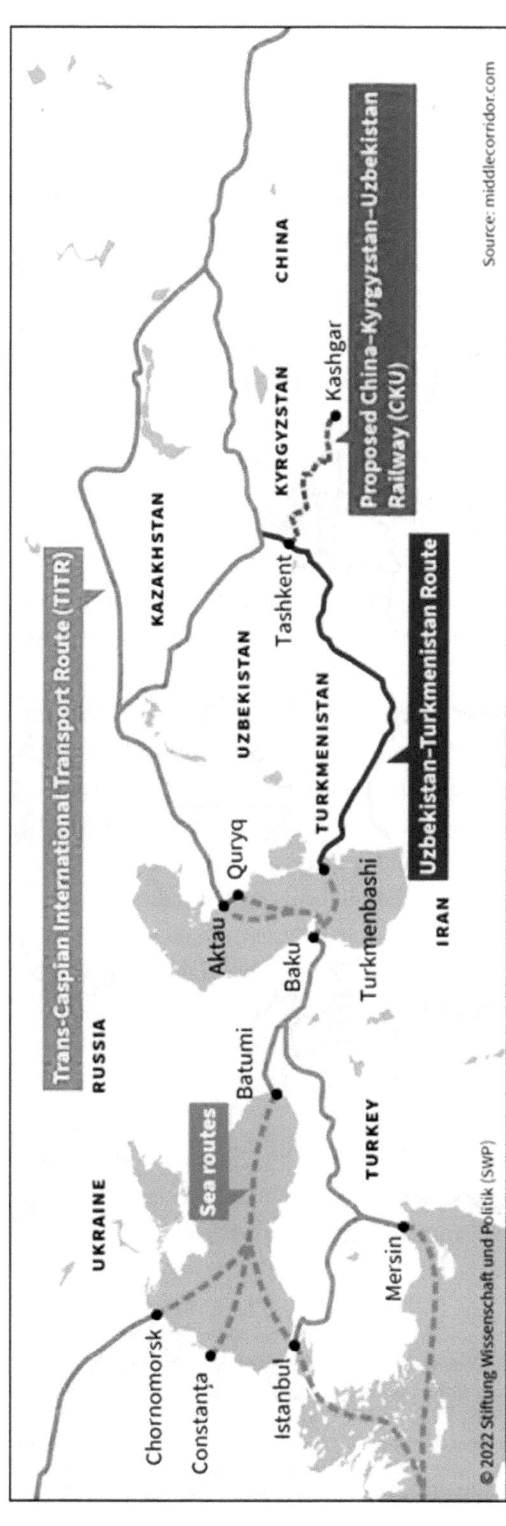

Map 6 Northern and Southern Variants of the Middle Corridor

Source: Middle Corridor, Trans-Caspian International Transport Route at www.middlecorridor.com (reprinted with permission).

terminus of the China-Pakistan Economic Corridor.[63] The new line will eventually not only offer easier access for Central Asian exporters to Chinese and Pakistani markets, but also promises future links to expanded domestic rail networks in the Kyrgyz Republic and Tajikistan.

In the longer term, currently difficult routes south of the Caspian Sea could be feasible. A route through Uzbekistan and Turkmenistan to Iran could connect to the Turkish rail network or to Iran's ocean ports, although US sanctions on Iran may be an obstacle for some potential customers. Afghanistan is a member of CAREC and several proposals aim to create an Afghan rail network or construct lines connecting Central Asia to Iran or Pakistan via Afghanistan. Although rail connections linking Central Asia to a southern network of Afghanistan, Iran and Pakistan are in the future, they are already on the agenda.[64]

The main lines of the Landbridge could be revived after the Russia-Ukraine war, if the post-war settlement is appropriate. What would be the impact on alternative routes? The Middle Corridor and services to Iran are already in use and will continue to attract traffic to and from Türkiye, the Middle East and North Africa, as well as Iran and southern Europe. The attractiveness of the alternative routes will be increased if the countries involved can reduce delays by simplifying customs procedures for trains in transit and prioritizing the through trains, by setting reasonable but not excessive freight rates, and by investing to improve choke points such as change of gauge.

Improved long-distance Eurasian rail services along the Middle Corridor or south of the Caspian Sea could provide an opportunity for the Central Asian countries to diversify beyond their limited export bundles by exporting manufactured or agri-food products and joining international supply chains. So far, the Central Asian countries have exported a narrow range of primary products and have been almost totally absent from international supply chains. Diversifying exports and becoming attractive supply chain partners will require domestic reforms to reduce the costs of doing business in general and of international trade in particular.

The rapid evolution of the Landbridge highlighted the importance of appropriate connectivity for international supply chains. The Landbridge remained robust to potential threats of disruption in 2014 and 2020, but the Russia-Ukraine war in

---

[63] China is making Kashi into a rail hub for western China. The Kashi-Hotan line opened in 2010 and the 825-km Hotan-Ruoqiang line that opened in 2022 completed the connection to Golmud, a major junction on the Xining-Lhasa line and with lines to Dunhuang (Gansu) and Chengdu. China is committed to a line from Kashi through Pakistan to the Indian Ocean as a planned element of the China Pakistan Economic Corridor.

[64] The rail links are often preceded by road links. The Karakorum Highway from Kashi to Pakistan has been in use for years, albeit with seasonal closures and often difficult conditions, and truck convoys have linked Uzbekistan to Kashi along a new road following a potential rail route.

2022 highlighted the dangers of relying on a system with a chokepoint (i.e. transiting Russia). The rapid response to war-driven disruption reflected the demand for transit services and the potential win-win gains for service providers as well as customers. Moreover, the long-term prospects for rail freight are positive; electric trains along well-maintained tracks are a more environmentally friendly mode of international transport than ships or aircraft.[65]

The geopolitical implications of the shift from the northern Landbridge line in Map 4 to the Middle Corridor and its Southern Variant (Maps 5 and 6) are clear. The dominance of rail routes running north to Russia will be reduced and new exports from Central Asia using the Middle Corridor will be travelling east or west rather than to the north.

5 Looking Forward

Central Asia's absorption into the Russian Empire and place in the Soviet Union showed striking continuity with respect to external boundaries and political control. Boundaries with Iran, Afghanistan and China have been essentially unchanged since the late 1800s, and political control was exerted by Russia until 1991. Economic relations were, however, strikingly different between the two eras. In the Tsarist Empire, Central Asia played a colonial role in supplying primary products to the metropole while Russia provided administration and infrastructure to support economic links and military control. In the Soviet era, Central Asia was part of a unified and highly integrated planned economy and of a multicultural union dedicated in principle to improving the living standards of all Soviet citizens. The differences were important in determining Central Asian reactions to the breakdown of the Tsarist Empire and of the Soviet Union.

In 1916 protests in Central Asia preceded and helped set the stage for the revolutions of 1917, and opposition to the new regime continued for a decade and longer. However, the longest lasting Central Asian response, that of the Basmachi, was essentially a pre-modern reaction to demands by foreign rulers and to immigrants into the region. The opposition to collectivization and sedentarization in Kazakhstan in the 1930s was also a response to challenges to a premodern lifestyle. In such cases, the protesters had little chance against the modern state. The protests were not helped by an absence of educated leaders; the Jadidists had limited impact in the 1910s and 1920s and their leaders would be executed in the 1930s to be replaced by more reliable Soviet-educated officials.

---

[65] Air freighting a 12,000-kilogram load from Chengdu to inland Western Europe produces about 54 tonnes of carbon dioxide, shipping by maritime and rail routes produces 3.3 tonnes, and rail-freighting across the Landbridge produces 2.8 tonnes. Regulations to reduce sulfur and other emissions between 2020 and 2050 will add to the cost of maritime freight (Pomfret, 2024).

The Soviet era left a mixed economic and social legacy. The improvement in indicators such as literacy rates or life expectancy from the 1920s to the 1980s was massive, as was the upgrading of many aspects of material living standards. The regime had some success in combining the creation of *homo sovieticus* (the new man of Soviet society) with pride in national status (at least for ethnic groups with their own republic). At the same time, there were outbreaks of anti-Russian behaviour and an underlying sense that, however benevolent the regime might be, Central Asia was being exploited for its natural resources.

In 1991, there was little appetite for independence but the opportunity to create nation states was seized after the dissolution of the Soviet Union. The national leaders consolidated personal power, creating super-presidential political systems and enjoying the benefits that accompanied autocratic rule. The leaders were also, to varying degrees, able to appeal to national consciousness through language, religion, and history that long predated Russian influence, which for most of the region dated back no more than 125 years.

While cementing political independence after 1991, the leaders were aware of the limits to economic independence, given the region's narrow specialization in the unified Soviet economy and tight economic links to Russia. Some primary product exports could find new markets quickly (e.g. cotton or gold), while other exports were constrained by inherited infrastructure (e.g. natural gas and oil) and were often part of supply chains that led to Russia. During the 1990s, diversification of economic partners proceeded slowly but steadily as dependence on Russia declined.

The global resource boom that started around the turn of the century was transformative. World prices for oil (and gas) and for minerals such as copper or gold rose rapidly. Construction of new pipelines for oil and gas became economically feasible and energy exports switched from dependence on Russian markets and pipelines in the 1990s to Europe and China as the primary markets in the 2010s. Improved transport infrastructure and diversification of routes have been a theme of the twenty-first century in Central Asia; the Russia-Ukraine war and accompanying sanctions highlighted the significance of infrastructure choice as EU-China rail freight started to shift from the northern Landbridge through Russia to Middle Corridor routes that ran west-east across Central Asia between the Caspian Sea and China, with support from the EU.[66]

---

[66] Tsereteli (2023, 1) emphasizes the importance of transport infrastructure for Central Asia and the incomplete process of upgrading non-Russian corridors: 'Strong leadership and continuous intense coordination between state and private actors will be required to address existing bottlenecks in the transportation system, and to increase commercial attractiveness of the transit corridor'.

The foreign policy counterpart of these economic changes was multi-vector diplomacy, emphasizing the variety of partners while downplaying the reduced role of Russia. The increased US interest in Central Asia during military operations in Afghanistan provided a new vector after 2001, although US interest subsided after 2014. At crucial points, such as recognition of Abkhazia and South Ossetia in 2008 or of Russia's annexation of Crimea in 2014, all five Central Asian countries withheld support for Russia. A similar position in 2022 after the Russian invasion of Ukraine was even clearer. The Central Asian countries have good reason to stand by the UN principle of respecting territorial integrity of UN member countries, and they have tacit support from China.

Since the resource boom, the Central Asian countries have been reforming their economic strategies in the direction of greater diversification of output and trade. Such change is slow because reforms may be resisted and after introduction of pro-enterprise or trade-facilitating measures the response can take time. Nevertheless, in the 2020s there are examples of domestic entrepreneurs and foreign investors identifying areas of competitive advantage and a wide range of markets, as well as of the emergence of logistics and other companies providing services to support imports of best-practice inputs and new exports.[67]

In November 2022 the French Development Agency published a booklet that included a map captioned 'Central Asia: Hub for Eurasian Overland Trade' (Levystone, 2022). Some of the spokes (e.g. the China-Pakistan Economic Corridor) have yet to be completed, some (e.g. the railway line from Tehran through eastern Türkiye) are in poor shape, and some 'under negotiation' are highly controversial (e.g. the Zangezur/Syunik corridor linking Azerbaijan and Turkey), but the big picture is striking. Central Asia can become a key link in Eurasian overland trade, again after a 500-year break. The original rail Landbridge through Kazakhstan and Russia will remain significant, and a southern Iran-Pakistan connection could carry some traffic, but Central Asia is at the heart of east-west trade. The old north-south lines from the Russian Empire and Soviet Union remain important. Central Asia will be the crossroads.

In the 2020s, the more assertive economic independence is reinforced by a new generation of leaders less moulded by Soviet experience and more willing

---

[67] At the October 2023 Silk Road Forum in Tbilisi, a CAREC session on value chains included presentations by (1) the area manager of a Singapore company that bought Central Asian production facilities in fertilizers, pharmaceuticals, and other products and exported to eastern Europe and the Middle East, (2) the CEO of an integrated cotton textile company in Uzbekistan that imported equipment from suppliers in East Asia, Europe, and North America and exported textiles and apparel to a wide range of countries, (3) a Kyrgyz businesswoman who organized tailors using imported inputs from China to make clothing for export to Kazakhstan, Russia, and Uzbekistan, and (4) the CEO of a logistics company based in Almaty that handled worldwide import supply. In all four cases, the mix was reporting solid success and foreseeing a positive future.

to cooperate within Central Asia. The Central Asian Five now look out to a wider world than the post-Soviet space. They are comfortable with China and the EU as major economic partners, and with partners from South Asia, Iran, Türkiye, Japan, South Korea, and elsewhere, and with speaking at the United Nations General Assembly and other international fora. The contrast in age and outlook between the first and the current generation of leaders and officials is matched in the wider population, where the average age is under thirty; a majority of the Central Asian population was born after the dissolution of the Soviet Union, and many more have no recollection of that era of Russian hegemony. Russia under current leadership may not like these developments but is in no position to reverse its declining influence in Central Asia.

Note on Abbreviations

$ refers to US dollars. The abbreviation EU applies to the European Union created in the 1993 Maastricht Treaty and its predecessors since 1957.

Glossary of International Agreements since 1991

Central Asian leaders joined the Commonwealth of Independent States after the dissolution of the Soviet Union. They signed many agreements in the 1990s and 2000s but were unwilling to countenance limits on national sovereignty and most agreements before the EAEU were paper agreements without significant impact. In the 1990s, all five countries joined the United Nations, International Monetary Fund and World Bank, but only the Kyrgyz Republic joined the World Trade Organization (in 1998). Tajikistan joined the WTO in 2013 and Kazakhstan in 2015; at the time of writing, Uzbekistan and Turkmenistan are negotiating WTO accession.

CIS   Commonwealth of Independent States dates from 1991 as an organization intended to maintain links between the twelve non-Baltic former Soviet republics with a secretariat in Moscow. The CIS has been a vehicle for bilateral free trade agreements or visa-free travel. Implementation has generally been weak.

EAEU   Eurasian Economic Union grew out of a customs union between Russia, Belarus, and Kazakhstan that was established in 2010. The EAEU was launched in 2015 as a deeper economic integration, with Armenia and the Kyrgyz Republic as additional members. The EAEU Commission is based in Moscow and the Court in Minsk.

The Eurasian Economic Community (the Union of Five) was an ineffective predecessor that included Tajikistan and briefly Uzbekistan. The Central Asian Economic Community (1998–2002) and the Central Asia Cooperation Organization (2002–5) were little more than paper agreements.

ECO Economic Cooperation Organization expanded in 1992, when the Central Asian countries and Azerbaijan joined original members Iran, Pakistan, and Turkey, to cover all major non-Arab Muslim countries west of India. The ECO Secretariat is in Tehran. Despite initial fanfare, ECO has had little impact.

SCO Shanghai Cooperation Organization was the successor to the Shanghai Forum in which China, Russia, Kazakhstan, Kyrgyzstan, and Tajikistan negotiated border demarcation between the former Soviet republics and China. With Uzbekistan's participation in 2001, the name SCO was adopted. In 2017, India and Pakistan became SCO members.

Belarus, Iran, and Mongolia have observer status. The annual summits are mostly attended by national leaders and often include invited guests (Azerbaijan, Turkey, and Turkmenistan in 2022, when the represented countries constituted almost half of the world's population). The SCO secretariat is in Beijing.

CAREC Central Asian Regional Economic Cooperation conceived in 2001 as a partnership between the Central Asian countries and six multilateral agencies (Asian Development Bank, European Bank for Reconstruction and Development, Islamic Development Bank, International Monetary Fund, United Nations Development Programme, and World Bank), country membership has expanded to include China, Afghanistan, Pakistan, Mongolia, Azerbaijan, and Georgia. The primary work of CAREC has been to coordinate trade and customs policies at the level of senior officials. The CAREC Secretariat is in Manila and the CAREC Institute is in Urumqi.

References and Further Reading

Arvis, Jean-François, Corduka Rastogi, and Daniel Saslavsky (2022): Effects on Global Logostics and Connectivity Effects, in Michele Ruta, ed., *The Impact of the War in Ukraine on Global Trade and Investment* (World Bank: Washington DC), 39–43.

Arynov, Zhanibek (2023): Discursive Delegitimation of the Eurasian Economic Union by the European Union, *Working Paper N° 54*, Institut Français d'Etudes sur l'Asie Centrale, Paris.

Benson, Linda (1990): *The Ili Rebellion: The Moslem Challenge to Chinese Authority in Xinjiang, 1944–1949* (M.E. Sharpe: Armonk).

Bradford, Anu (2020): *The Brussels Effect: How the European Union Rules the World* (Oxford University Press: New York).

Brophy, David (2016): *Uygur Nation: Reform and Revolution on the Russia-China Frontier* (Harvard University Press: Cambridge MA).

Brower, Daniel (2003): *Turkestan and the Fate of the Russian Empire* (Routledge: London).

Cameron, Sarah (2018): *The Hungry Steppe: Famine, Violence, and the Making of Soviet Kazakhstan* (Cornell University Press: Ithaca NY).

Chokobaeva, Aminat, Chloé Drieu, and Alexander Morrison, eds. (2020): *The Central Asian Revolt of 1916: A Collapsing Empire in the Age of War and Revolution* (Manchester University Press: Manchester).

Chupilkin, Maxim, Beata Javorcik, and Alexander Plekhanov (2023): The Eurasian Roundabout: Trade Flows into Russia through the Caucasus and Central Asia, *EBRD Working Paper No. 276*, European Bank for Reconstruction and Development, London.

Cooley, Alexander, and John Heathershaw (2019): *Dictators without Borders: Power and Money in Central Asia* (Yale University Press: New Haven CT).

Edgar, Adrienne (2004): *Tribal Nation: The Making of Soviet Turkmenistan* (Princeton University Press: Princeton NJ).

European Bank for Reconstruction and Development (2023): *Sustainable Transport Connections between Europe and Central Asia*, Final Report 16 June (EBRD: London).

Global Witness (2006): *It's a Gas: Funny Business in the Turkmen-Ukraine Gas Trade* (Global Witness: Washington DC).

Hellie, Richard (1971): *Enserfment and Military Change in Muscovy* (University of Chicago Press: Chicago IL).

Hellie, Richard (1982): *Slavery in Russia, 1450–1725* (University of Chicago Press: Chicago IL).

Hellie, Richard (1999): *The Economy and Material Culture of Russia, 1660–1725* (University of Chicago Press: Chicago IL).

Hopkirk, Peter (1990): *The Great Game* (Oxford University Press: Oxford).

Hugot, Jules, and Roman Mogilevskii (2023): The Economic Impact of the Russian Invasion of Ukraine on the Caucasus and Central Asia: Short-Term Benefits and Long- Term Challenges, *Asian Development Outlook*, April, 34–39.

Kaminski, Bartlomiej, and Saumya Mitra (2012): *Borderless Bazaars and Regional Integration in Central Asia: Emerging Patterns of Trade and Cross-Border Cooperation* (World Bank: Washington DC).

Kamp, Marianne (2006): *The New Woman in Uzbekistan: Islam, Modernity and Unveiling under Communism*. University of Washington Press: Seattle, WA .

Kamp, Marianne, and Niccolò Pianciola (2022): Collectivisation, Sedentarisation and Famine in Central Asia, in Rico Isaacs and Erica Marat, eds., *Routledge Handbook of Contemporary Central Asia* (Routledge: London), 41–55.

Kassymbekova, Botakoz (2016): *Despite Cultures: Early Soviet Rule in Tajikistan* (University of Pittsburgh Press: Pittsburgh PA).

Keller, Shoshana (2020): *Russia and Central Asia: Coexistence, Conquest, Convergence* (University of Toronto Press: Toronto).

Khalid, Adeeb (2021): *Central Asia: A New History from the Imperial Conquests to the Present* (Princeton University Press: Princeton NJ).

Khitakhunov, Azimzhan (2021): *The Risks of Corruption: The Case of Central Asia*, Eurasian Research Institute, Ahmet Yesevi Turkish-Kazakh University, Almaty – www.eurasian-research.org/publication/the-risks-of-corruption-the-case-of-central-asia/ and https://research.hktdc.com/en/article/Nzc3MjQ5Nzk0.

Levi, Scott (2020): *The Bukharan Crisis: A Connected History of 18th Century Central Asia* (University of Pittsburgh Press: Pittsburgh PA).

Levystone, Michaël (2022): Connectivity in Central Asia at the Crossroads of International Crises: Transport, Energy and Water from Interdependence to New Cooperation Ways, *Russie.Nei.Reports*, No. 41, Institut Français des Relations Internationales (Ifri), Paris.

Mankoff, Jeffrey (2022): *Empires of Eurasia: How Imperial Legacies Shape International Security* (Yale University Press: New Haven CT).

Martin, Terry (2001): *The Affirmative Action Empire: Nations and Nationalism in the Soviet Union* (Cornell University Press: Ithaca NY).

Michaels, Paula (2003): *Curative Powers: Medicine and Empire in Stalin's Soviet Central Asia* (University of Pittsburgh Press: Pittsburgh PA).

Mogilevskii, Roman (2012): Trends and Patterns in Foreign Trade of Central Asian Countries. *Institute of Public Policy Working Paper*, 1/2012, University of Central Asia Bishkek.

Monteiro-Benson, Misha (2023): Will Kazakhstan's Brain Drain Become a Wartime Brain Gain? *East Asia Forum*, 11 October.

Morrison, Alexander (2012): Metropole, Colony, and Imperial Citizenship in the Russian Empire, *Kritika: Explorations in Russian and Eurasian History* 13(2), 327–64.

Northrop, Douglas (2004): *Veiled Empire* (Cornell University Press: Ithaca NY).

Nyman, Lars-Erik (1977): *Great Britain and Chinese, Russian and Japanese Interests in Sinkiang, 1918–1934, Lund Studies in International History No.8* (Esselte Studium: Stockholm).

Obertreis, Julia (2017): *Imperial Desert Dreams: Cotton Growing and Irrigation in Central Asia, 1860–1991* (V&R unipress: Göttingen).

Pianciola, Niccolo (2018): Ukraine and Kazakhstan: Comparing the Famines – Contribution to the Famine Roundtable, *Contemporary European History* 27(3), 460–64.

Pomfret, Richard (1995): *The Economies of Central Asia* (Princeton University Press: Princeton NJ; paperback edition, print on demand, Princeton Legacy Library, 2014).

Pomfret, Richard (2006): *The Central Asian Economies since Independence* (Princeton University Press: Princeton NJ).

Pomfret, Richard (2019): *The Central Asian Economies in the Twenty-first Century: Paving a New Silk Road* (Princeton University Press: Princeton NJ) – Uzbek translation *21-Asrda Markaziy Osiyo Davlatlari Iqtisodiyoti: Yangi ipak yo'lining paydo bo'lishi* (Yuridik Adabiyotlar: Tashkent, forthcoming).

Pomfret, Richard (2021): Central Asian Economies Thirty Years after Dissolution of the Soviet Union, *Comparative Economic Studies* 63(4), 537–56.

Pomfret, Richard (2023): What Did Those Who Were 'Present at the Transition' Miss? The Creation of Powerful Presidential Families in Central Asia, *Comparative Economic Studies* 65(3), 442–60.

Pomfret, Richard (2024): Rail Transport Corridors in the CAREC Region: Long-Term Supply Chain Resilience and Short-Term Shocks, in Dina Azhgaliyeva, ed., *Transport Corridors in CAREC Region: Trade Facilitation and Supply Chain Resilience* (Asian Development Bank Institute: Tokyo).

Smele, Jonathan (2015): *The 'Russian' Civil Wars, 1916–1926: Ten Years that Shook the World* (Hurst: London).

Stronski, Paul (2010): *Tashkent: Forging a Soviet city, 1930–1966* (University of Pittsburgh Press: Pittsburgh PA).

Tsereteli, Mamuka (2023): The Strategic Value of Connectivity in Central Asia and the Caucasus, *Central Asia-Caucasus Analyst*, 15 September.

Wheatcroft, Stephen (2021): The Complexity of the Kazakh Famine: Food Problems and Faulty Perceptions (critical review of Cameron, 2018), *Journal of Genocide Research* 23(4), 593–97.

Wilde, Andreas (2012): *What Is Beyond the River? Power, Authority and Social Order in Eighteenth and Nineteenth Century Transoxania* (University of Bonn: Bonn).

Yuldasheva, Guli (2013): The Northern Distribution Network and Central Asia, in Andris Sprūds and Diāna Potjomkina, eds., *Northern Distribution Network: Redefining Partnerships within NATO and beyond* (Latvian Institute of International Affairs: Riga), 93–113.

Zhao, Chengfan (2023): *China-Europe Trains in 2022; East-West Imbalance and Drops in Volume*, www.railfreight.com/beltandroad/2023/02/15/china-europe-trains-in-2022-east-west-imbalance-and-drops-in-volume/ 15 February 2023 (accessed 17 October 2023).

Acknowledgements

I am grateful to the editors, two anonymous reviewers, and Eugene Finkel for helpful comments on a first draft.

Printed by Libri Plureos GmbH in Hamburg,
Germany